Frederic William Farrar

Inspiration.

Frederic William Farrar

Inspiration.

ISBN/EAN: 9783337183363

Printed in Europe, USA, Canada, Australia, Japan

Cover: Foto ©Lupo / pixelio.de

More available books at **www.hansebooks.com**

INSPIRATION.

A Clerical Symposium

ON

*"IN WHAT SENSE, AND WITHIN WHAT LIMITS,
IS THE BIBLE THE WORD OF GOD?"*

BY

THE VEN. ARCHDEACON FARRAR,
PRINCIPAL CAIRNS,
PREBENDARY STANLEY LEATHES,
REV. EDWARD WHITE,
AND OTHERS.

NEW YORK:
THOMAS WHITTAKER,
2 AND 3 BIBLE HOUSE.
1885.

PREFACE.

WRITERS, representing various sections of the Church, have skilfully and devoutly stated, in the pages of the *Homiletic Magazine*, their convictions on the subject of Inspiration. The question of the meaning and extent of the Inspiration of the Sacred Volume, is one that underlies almost all other theological questions. It has therefore been deemed advisable to send forth, in a compact form, the whole series of papers, which make a contribution to theological science, at once valuable for scholarship and fairness.

FREDERICK HASTINGS,
Editor of Homiletic Magazine (late Quarterly.)

LONDON, 1884.

CONTENTS.

ARTICLE	PAGE
I. REV. PROF. J. RADFORD THOMSON, M.A.	1
II. REV. PREBENDARY STANLEY LEATHES, D.D.	23
III. REV. PRINCIPAL JOHN CAIRNS, D.D.	48
IV. REV. ALEXANDER MACKENNAL, M.A.	66
V. REV. PAGE HOPPS	79
VI. REV. W. CROSBY BARLOW, M.A.	93
VII. REV. PROF. G. W. OLVER, M.A.	119
VIII. REV. EDWARD WHITE	137
XI. PROF. ISRAEL ABRAHAMS, M.A.	155
X. RIGHT REV. BISHOP WEATHERS	175
XI. VEN. ARCHDEACON FARRAR, D.D.	202

SYMPOSIUM ON INSPIRATION.

"IN WHAT SENSE, AND WITHIN WHAT LIMITS, IS THE BIBLE TO BE REGARDED AS THE WORD OF GOD?"

ARTICLE I.

BY THE REV. PROF. RADFORD THOMSON, M.A.

THE Bible may be made the basis of two completely different arguments. If the existence of a Divine Governor of the Universe be the question under consideration, the sacred volume, as an actual fact and as a moral power, may fairly be adduced as an evidence of a supernatural interposition and guidance. On the other hand, if the Divine existence and rule be acknowledged, it is allowable to bring forward the Book, and to ask whether it bears such marks as entitle it to be deemed in some special sense the workmanship of the eternal mind. It is rather under this latter aspect that I am asked to view the Scriptures in this friendly symposium.

In thinking and writing upon this theme, it is

impossible not to feel how different is the treatment the Bible meets with in our own days, from that to which it was subjected in days gone by. We may almost say, the Bible has no enemies, and if it has critics, they are all friendly critics, anxious to say all they sincerely can say in its favour. Prof. Matthew Arnold represents modern literature, and is often regarded as one of the severest critics of the current Christianity; yet he says: "As well imagine a man with a sense for sculpture not cultivating it by the help of the remains of Greek art, or a man with a sense for poetry not cultivating it by the help of Homer and Shakespeare, as a man with a sense for conduct not cultivating it by the help of the Bible." Professor Huxley represents modern science, and is the *bête noire* of controversial theologians; yet he says: "I have been perplexed to know by what practical measures the religious feeling, which is the essential basis of conduct, was to be kept up . . . without the use of the Bible." No doubt, both these gentlemen would dissent from the declaration of the late Dr. Tregelles, who professed that to him all the 66 books of Scripture were entirely and in every part as if written by the pen of God Himself. Yet they would, certainly one of them, perhaps both, acknowledge the Bible to be the Word of God, were they permitted to describe the Eternal in their own way. Among the ignorant and the vulgar there are still to be found vituperators of Scripture and blasphemers; but in literature, in society, we meet with nothing but cordial appreciation. This is owing to the joint influence of enlightenment and liberty, which naturally bring charity and candour in their train. There is no dispute as to the fact that some of the Scripture writers were men of genius; that their tone of moral thinking and teaching was far higher than prevailed elsewhere in the ancient world: and that the Book, as a whole, has been the source of social blessings and the inspiration of social progress. Making allowance for human fallibility and eliminating all the miraculous as incredible, but as written with no purpose to deceive, the Bible would probably be acknowledged, by almost all contemporary thinkers of any credit, to be the most wonderful and the best Book the world has seen.

But we shall make a great mistake if we suppose that there is anything approaching to a general agreement among educated and thoughtful Englishmen as to what the Bible is. What is it generally regarded as being? In reading the other day the last volume of Bishop Wilberforce's life, I came upon, and made a note of, a passage which I will here quote. The belief of the late Bishop Wilberforce was, I think, a fair representation of the belief of orthodox and educated English Christians generally. "In brief," says he,* "my belief is this:—The whole Bible comes to us as 'the Word of God' under the sanction of God the Holy Ghost." We cannot pick and choose amidst its contents; all is God's Word to us. But as I believe that this, which I hold as the only orthodox view, is encompassed by many difficulties by what is called the theory of Verbal Inspiration, I desired to show how, in my judgment, a careful scrutiny of the Bible revealed the divers manners in which the Holy Ghost spake:—

"I. Sometimes by the mere mechanical use of the human agent who conveyed the message, as when (1) God wrote words on the first tables; (2) dictated them for the second; or (3) committed them to prophets simply to repeat; or (4) spake them through the prophets.

"II. Sometimes by possessing the human instrument with a complete knowledge of that he was to speak, and leaving him to express it under the mere suggestions and guardianship of His own special presence according to the natural use of the

* "Life of the Right Rev. S. Wilberforce, D.D.," vol. iii., pp. 149, 150.

human faculties. I desired, I say, to show how this would greatly lessen these difficulties, and enable men to realise the essential differences between Holy Scripture and any other books; namely that, as all truth comes from God, other books may be in a sense said to be inspired because they are true, but Holy Scripture alone can be affirmed to be true because it is inspired."

Such definitions as that of Bishop Wilberforce belong to a reflective and critical age. Yet that in some sense the Bible has from the beginning been deemed a sacred book is not disputed. Clement of Rome calls the Scriptures, " the true words of the Holy Ghost." According to Westcott, " The first simple collective title of the whole Bible appears to be that which is found in Jerome in the 4th century, the Divine Library (Bibliotheca Divina)."* Perhaps many minds would prefer to rest in such simple and vague statements as these. But it is not possible or desirable to evade questions which do and will start up, when minds are active, inquiries are general, and doubts are wide-spread.

My own temptation, I admit, is not so much to " level down " the Scriptures to other manifestations of Deity, as, on the contrary, to " level up " these

* " The Bible in the Church," p. 5.

latter to become a Divine Revelation. Without confusing God with Nature, I delight to see God in Nature. To me, the blue crocus that is opening before my eye in the sunshine of this February morning, the yellow jessamine that brightens my library window, are a word from God. Much more the sweet and trustful expression of my child, who just now came to know if he could do anything for me before going to school. Can I then doubt whether the story of the Saviour blessing the babes, which I read to my assembled household at prayers this morning, was a word from God? To my own mind such doubt is impossible. But the question is not as to the Divine origin of Scripture, so much as to the sense in which, the limits within which, the Bible is God's Word. It is a question for the understanding, to resolve which needs not merely spiritual perception, but logical acuteness and discrimination. To make my judgment plain and definite, I answer :—

The Bible is the Word of God : (1) inasmuch as it is constructed upon a plan, and a plan which only Divine Wisdom could devise and carry out; (2) inasmuch as it contains declarations, truths, which man could not make known, and which proceed from God; (3) inasmuch as its writers may reasonably be deemed to have been Divinely inspired;

and (4) inasmuch as its main purpose is to witness to One who is alone in the highest, the proper sense of the term, "The Word of God."

I. There is one respect in which, to a mind prepared to believe that God interests Himself in human well-being, the Bible must present marks of Divine action: the plan upon which the volume as a whole is constructed, and apparently has been designed, is such as human wisdom certainly could neither have arranged nor wrought out. Although written by very different authors, removed from one another by long centuries of time, and by changed conditions of society, it possesses a most singular unity,—a unity not of sameness, but of harmony; a unity of plan and orderly development,—an organic unity. There is no hiatus and no repetition; no part could be dispensed with,— no part could be inserted without spoiling the effect of the whole. This is an argument which can only be appreciated by a mind accustomed to historical survey, and an imagination cultivated by familiarity with works of art. But to such a mind it is very effective.

The growth of the historical spirit, and the influence exerted by the widely-accepted theory of Evolution, have done much both to modify the view of the Bible entertained by educated believers, and to enhance their admiration of the volume. It is no longer regarded as one book, or consulted in an indiscriminating way as a collection of oracles, every word in which is of equal authority with every other. It is rather thought of as an organic product, each part of which has a relation to the other parts; the whole of which was conceived in the Divine Mind, and wrought out gradually through long centuries. It is admitted that there is a development of religious doctrine, divinely guided, but still a development. The interest with which the Christian public has regarded such books as those of Dr. Newman Smyth, Dr. Bruce, and Mr. Adeney, is a proof that such a view meets a want in the minds of men of this age. And just as the theory of development in nature, if opposed, must be opposed on scientific and not on theological grounds, and is regarded by those theologians who accept it as a most powerful proof of the operation of a supernatural mind and will,—so with the Scriptures. Their growth unto perfection reveals to those who believe in God, the presiding care, the consummate wisdom, the marvellous goodness of Him whose progressive Revelation corresponds to the progressive growth of the spiritual humanity.

II. It is generally admitted by those who believe in God in any other sense than as "The Unknowable," that there are in three spheres valuable and trustworthy manifestations of the Divine. God is revealed in Nature; for Sir William Hamilton's paradox that Nature conceals God can hardly be taken seriously. He is revealed in Conscience, in man's moral nature, judgments and sentiments, as St. Paul shows so plainly in the Epistle to the Romans. And further, there is a special revelation to certain human spirits summoned to an intimate intercourse with the Father of Spirits, such as was the case with the inspired writers of Scripture.

Many religions have their sacred books: Brahminism has its Vedas, Parseeism has the Zendavesta, Confucianism the writings of the Chinese sage, and Mohammedanism its Koran.

Doubtless the prevalent tendency at the present time is to rest the claims of the Bible to a Divine authority upon the intrinsic excellence, at all events, of the greater portion of the volume. It is, of course, a question how far testimony to the Divinity of the Scriptures is valuable which bases itself upon a spiritual appreciation of their adaptation to the higher needs of man. What shall we say of Dr. Edwin Abbott's evidence,* when after,

* *Modern Review*, October 1882.

as he thinks, disproving by the indirect testimony of Justin Martyr the claim of the fourth Gospel to be the work of an apostle, he yet approves its universal recognition in the early Church on the ground of "the intrinsic power of this most spiritual treatise," which "succeeded because it deserved to succeed, because it was, spiritually speaking, in accordance with the truth"?

The Bible is usually deemed by Christians the Word of God, because it contains a Revelation, and because it is the work of inspired men. Both Revelation and Inspiration are supernatural, and when they meet together, as they are believed to do in the structure and composition of the sacred volume, they impart to the work in which they co-operate a peculiar attribute of Divinity.

A critical generation like this is constrained to scrutinise claims to paramount excellence; and this is done sometimes in an irreverent, but sometimes also in a reverent spirit.

There is perhaps no reflective reader of Scripture who has not sometimes been tempted to question within himself whether the space has been as well occupied as might have been the case. Some optical students have been of opinion that if they had been consulted, the eye might have been better made than Nature, or the Creator, has made it.

But such criticism requires Omniscience to justify it. It is plain that the Author of the Universe has worked within His powers, and that He had reason for doing so; and perhaps the present disciplinary state of mankind is one reason. In reading the Synoptic Gospels I have sometimes, I confess, regretted the repetitions which abound in them, and have wished that instead of these there had been preserved some additional records of the Saviour's sayings and doings. In reading the Acts of the Apostles I have often regretted that the narrative of St. Paul's conversion should be told again and again, when there is so much that I should like to have known about the apostle, for which no room has been found. Parts of the Epistle to the Hebrews and parts of the Apocalypse have but little interest for us "sinners of the Gentiles." But a little reflection assures us that in such matters our wisdom may be foolishness; the Word, as a whole, doubtless appears harmonious and perfect to the mind of the All-wise. And there are not wanting glimmerings of an explanation in such cases which may encourage a submissive modesty.

I cannot but think that a decided conviction as to the reality of Revelation is of far greater importance than a theory of Inspiration. Dr. Newman

Smyth well says: "An affirmative and very positive answer may be given to the question, 'Have we a series or order of events and teaching which constitute a revelation from God?' while doubt and hesitancy may be felt in answering that other question, 'How was the Word of God made known, or what was the precise nature and degree of Inspiration?'"*

Now, Revelation seems to me to have been concentrated in two epochs; the time of Moses and the time of Christ. "The law was given by Moses, and grace and truth came by Jesus Christ." I do not mean to deny that Revelation has come otherwise; but mainly and pre-eminently it was accorded at those two crucial periods of the history of humanity. But Inspiration I conceive to have been far more diffused, and in very different degrees. I can see no Revelation in the books of Chronicles or Proverbs; but I can very well believe that some measure of inspiration was accorded to their writers, though a far higher degree of that impulse was necessary to the production of the Psalms and the prophecies of Isaiah.

It is plainly impossible that God should have communicated with man except within the limita-

* "Old Faiths in New Light."

tious imposed by human faculties; and it is no disparagement, but rather a high recommendation of "the Word," that it should come through human minds and human lips. Prof. Max Müller has justly said that "a revelation ready made and given to men like a language formed in heaven, would have been a foreign revelation that men could not understand." But we may go further than this, and say with Dr. Hannah :* "God's light loses nothing of its heavenly purity because it is reflected back from human faces; while man gains all the advantage of the pervading presence of a sympathy which answers to the most varied emotions of his heart."

Attention has often been drawn to the fact that there is an amazing difference of intrinsic value between the Canonical books of the New Testament and the Christian literature immediately succeeding. No one with any literary and spiritual discernment can question this. The First Epistle of Clement is a document of worth, but I imagine few would, with Mr. Matthew Arnold, rank it with the Second Epistle of Peter, or even with the Epistle of Jude. The apocryphal Gospels, the Shepherd of Hermas, &c., are not comparable with the books of the New Testament. The ortho-

* "Relation of Divine and Human Elements," p. 225.

dox interpretation of the difference seems to me the most reasonable:—" The apostolic period is not only a part of the history of the apprehension of truth by man; it is also a part of the history of the communication of truth by God."*

III. Within the circle of Christendom there are to be found opposite tendencies, both of which seem to me to disparage Scripture, yet neither of which questions that it is the Divine word to man.

There is, first, the mystical tendency, which exalts individual inspiration. All Christians admit with thankfulness that the Holy Spirit within is a Spirit of inspiration, disposing to appreciate and respond to the Divine Revelation from without; but the mystics seem to me to come very near to making the indwelling Spirit a Spirit not only of inspiration, but of revelation. If this be so, there does not appear to be any distinctive sense in which the Bible is God's Word, for no one knows whether or not his neighbour is equally qualified to reveal Divine Truth.

There is, in the second place, the "Catholic" tendency, which exalts the Church at the expense of the Bible, and which seems especially objectionable, not as abolishing "finality" (for we all

* Bernard, "The Progress of Doctrine," p. 13.

believe that "the Lord has yet more light and truth to break forth from His word"), but rather as putting a new patch upon an old garment.

The relation of the Church to the Scriptures is a delicate and difficult question. Bishop Wordsworth,[*] who is a champion of the Protestant view, defines the functions of the Primitive Church in reference to Holy Scripture as those of (1) a Witness, (2) a Guardian, (3) a Herald, and (4) a Judge. Of course, it is upon the fourth point that controversy arises. "We do not hesitate to confess," says Bishop Wordsworth, "that we have received the Scriptures from God through the ministry of the Church. But the Scriptures are not the Word of the Church, but the Word of God. They owe their authority not to her, but to Him." If this is admitted, and I do not suppose divines of the Roman communion would deny it—still the question arises, how has the Church authenticated certain books as canonical? and when and where? It was done, I conceive, gradually and unconsciously, not, in the first place, on the ground of merit, but on the ground of the position of the writers; for the works of certain apostles and apostolic men would be and were reverently read in the Christian assemblies. "The idea of canoni-

[*] "The Inspiration of Holy Scripture."

city," says Dr. Robertson Smith, "the right of a book to be cited as Scripture, was closely connected with regular use in public worship, and so the first step towards a New Testament Canon was doubtless the establishment of a custom of reading in the Churches individual epistles and Gospels."* I am speaking, of course, of the New Testament. The books of the Old Covenant were read in the public assemblies of the early Church, whilst the New Testament Canon was still in process of formation. In fact, to quote Canon Westcott, "The idea of a New Testament, consisting of definite books, and equal in authority to the Old, was foreign to the sub-apostolic age. Such an idea was necessarily the growth of time." The immediate successors of the apostles did not perceive that the written memoirs of the Lord, and the scattered writings of His first disciples, would form a sure and sufficient source or test of doctrine when the current tradition had grown indistinct or corrupt."

The fact seems to be that the solid and permanent record and the fluid society support each other. It is only partisans who can base the Church on the Bible or the Bible on the Church. "The Church offered a living commentary on the

* Article "Bible," in Encyc. Brit.

Book, and the Book an unchanging test of the Church." The two have one and the same Divine origin. "The canon of Scripture cannot be made to rest upon the Church, for the Bible and the Church were both the simultaneous outgrowths of something which was in the world before them both,—they were the twin fruits of a life which was before them both."*

Is it necessary, in order to a firm belief in the Divine origin and authority of Scripture, to hold —what is very generally held—that its language often conveys a meaning not apprehended by the mind of the inspired penman? There is a maxim —"Nihil est in scripto, quod non prius in scriptore." This maxim is all very well for a logician, but it does not do for a poet, much less for a prophet. Great truths may be suggested by local and temporary circumstances, and those truths may require millenniums of history in which to work themselves out and display their harmony and completeness.

There is a view of inspiration which has been very prevalent among Broad Church thinkers during the last generation. I refer to that introduced by Coleridge, who held that whatever "finds" a spiritual nature, i.e., whatever, by reason of its

* Newman Smyth, pp. 51, 52.

goodness and moral beauty and power, lays hold of a man's soul, and does him good, is, in virtue of that potency, to be regarded as inspired. It is admitted that this is the case with parts of the Bible in a measure far beyond what can be asserted of any other literature. Bishop Harold Browne justly says that the adoption of this principle would set Baxter's "Saint's Everlasting Rest" above the Book of Chronicles; and I have no doubt this would be admitted by the adherents of the view in question.

One cannot believe that it required any very high degree of inspiration to write the Book of Ruth, for example. It would be contrary to the analogy of the faith to suppose that an unnecessary measure of inspiration was afforded in such a case. Perhaps not very much more was needed for such a work than for the construction of the tabernacle of the wilderness; perhaps not so much as for the writing of the "Pilgrim's Progress," or the "Christian Year." But what was needed was accorded. And when John wrote his Gospel, it is evident that the Spirit of Truth was accorded, as promised, so as to bring all things to his recollection and to lead him into all truth.

That the Bible is the word of men is not questioned. It is written in human language by human penmen, in the exercise of human imagination, feeling, and intellect. In fact, it is intensely human. In it men write about men and for men. Remembering the maxim, *Humanum est errare*, are we to admit that so human a volume as the Bible lacks one mark of human origin—a note never absent from the workmanship of man—I mean fallibility? My answer is, the Revelation from heaven is infallible; but the inspiration of those who convey the revelation does not prevent their communications to their fellow-men from participating in the infirmities of their own nature. There are undoubted errors, *e.g.*, of fact, of chronology, and of number, &c., in the Scriptures.

Upon this point, the existence in Scripture of the human element to such an extent as to admit of human error and infirmity, the judicious statement of Bishop Ellicott may be quoted: "In the case of the written Word, viewed on its purely human side, and in its reference to matters previously admitted to have no bearing on Divine Truth, we may admit therein the existence of such incompleteness, such limitations, and such imperfections as belong even to the highest forms of purely truthful *human* testimony; but consistently deny the existence of mistaken views, perversions, misrepresentation, and any form whatever of consciously committed error or inaccuracy."*

Mr. Warrington goes much farther than this, and, after a very careful and reverent examination of the sacred volume, gives it as his opinion, "That in regard to all historical statements of Scripture, regarded in their outward aspect, as narratives of matter of fact, the inspiration under which the sacred writers wrote left them entirely to themselves, both as to sources of information and accuracy of statement, neither directing, controlling, or authorising their statements in these particulars in any way whatever; for which historical statements so regarded, therefore, the human authors only are to be held responsible." †

IV. The Scriptures do not explicitly claim to be the Word of God, nor does any one of the books of which they are composed put forward this claim. Yet the expression is a Scriptural one; in the Old Testament we meet frequently with references to the word of the Lord, *i.e.*, of Jehovah or Jahveh, and in the New Testament the parallel phrase, the Word of God, is common. The word of the Lord came to the prophets. The words in

---

* "Aids to Faith," pp. 417, 418.
† "The Inspiration of Scripture," p. 238.

which Moses published the will of God to Israel were the words of the Lord. The Word of God came to John, the last of the prophets, as to his illustrious predecessors. It is, however, one thing for the assertion to be made that the word of the Lord came to this and that inspired man, and has been recorded in Scripture, and another thing for the assertion to be made that the Bible calls itself the Word of God. Mr. Warrington says that the phrase in question occurs three or four hundred times in the Old Testament, and a hundred times in the New, but is never once applied to Scripture itself.*

But I consider this designation to be supremely applicable to Holy Scripture, inasmuch as in my view the main purpose of the Bible, from beginning to end, is to testify to Him who is the Son of God and the Saviour of mankind. The Bible is a problem of which the solution is—Christ.

The Word of God is emphatically the living Christ; not His spoken utterances so much as Himself, manifesting, as He does, the mind and heart of the Supreme. John especially delights so to designate Him, both in His pre-existent glory and in His victorious reign.

A parallel has often been drawn between the

* "The Inspiration of Scripture," Appendix.

Scriptures and the Christ in respect of the union of the Divine and human in both. It has been said that as in our Saviour there is a combination of two natures, as He is both Son of God and Son of man, so likewise has the Bible a human shape and substance, which is nevertheless informed, animated, and glorified by the indwelling Divine Spirit. But it cannot be maintained that the writers of the books of the Bible were as obedient and responsive to the Holy Spirit, as perfectly free from all independent volition, as the human nature of Christ was lost in the indwelling Word that used that nature as a pliant instrument, a perfect vehicle.

If God was to speak to men, I believe He could not have spoken with fulness and clearness otherwise than in the person and mediation of His Son. A "book revelation" alone would have been no revelation. But the book is the record, the witness, the herald of One greater even than itself. And the Scriptures are Divine because they are *the word of the Word.*

Article II.

BY THE REV. PREBDY. STANLEY LEATHES, D.D.

MANY years ago, in the *Essays and Reviews* controversy, distinction was very carefully drawn between the statement, that the Bible was the Word of God and that it contained the Word of God. Those who advocated the latter position laid great stress upon the wording of the Sixth Article of the English Church: "Holy Scripture *containeth* all things necessary to salvation," &c., seeking thereby to gain a most unfair advantage from a merely accidental verbal resemblance between the article and their thesis, inasmuch as to press the word "*containeth*" was hardly more reasonable than to press the words "*Holy Scripture*" on the other side, seeing that Scripture is not holy except as being derived from God, and that if it is written, it is presumably written because so derived. The attempt to argue any such controversy on the terms of the received formularies was inherently absurd and unsound, inasmuch as when they were framed the distinction had not been thought of, and therefore could not have been anticipated or provided for by any human language. Whether or not the distinction is in itself a valid one is another matter, which must be determined on its own merits, and not with reference to the accidental terminology of the English Church. Suppose it is admitted in all good faith that the Bible *contains* the Word of God. Then scattered up and down the Bible somewhere we may suppose that there is something which may rightly be regarded as the Word of God. Opinions will undoubtedly vary as to what and where these elements may be, but that they do exist and are to be found is undeniably true, if the admission that the Bible *contains* the Word of God is made in all good faith. Practically, however, there is a difficulty arising out of this position which has the effect of reducing the admission to a nullity. For if the Bible contains the Word of God, so that every individual must discern it for himself, then seeing that no two individuals may agree as to the particular elements which are the Word of God, we are landed in this dilemma,—either that there is no absolute Word of God at all, which all may acknowledge, or else that whatever strikes each individual in turn as the Word of God is to *him* the Word of God, but to him alone, except so far as others may happen to agree with him. There can, therefore, be no question that to affirm of the Bible that it contains the Word of God, in contradistinction to its being the Word of God, is very nearly tantamount to affirming that we have no actual Word of God at all, at least such as all may readily acknowledge, unless, in addition to saying that the Bible contains the Word of God, we go on to say also in what way we may determine what is or is not the Word of God. On the other hand, it is clearly undeniable that if we are to accept the Bible on its own terms, we shall be obliged to confess that it comes to us with Divine authority, as not only containing a Divine message, but as being in some sense the very embodiment of that message.

In what sense, then, and within what limits, is that true? We cannot ask the question without seeing also that the further question of canonicity is very largely involved in that concerning the Divine message; into the question, however, we cannot enter, we must accept the usual limits of the Old and New Testaments as sufficiently correct and intelligible for all practical purposes. How then, speaking generally, does the Bible commend itself to us as the Word of God, and in what sense does it so commend itself? In the first place, the

New Testament, beyond all question, claims and assumes that honour for the Old. We may take that for granted, and need not stop to prove it. The New Testament, as a matter of fact, claims an authority for the Old Testament which neither in gospels nor epistles it makes for itself. As a matter of fact, whether rightly or wrongly, the position assigned to the Old Testament by the New is very much that with which the Bible at large is regarded by religious people. Our Lord taught us that not one jot or tittle should pass from the Law till all was fulfilled, that the Scriptures of the prophets must be fulfilled, that all things that were written in the Law of Moses, and in the prophets, and in the Psalms, concerning Him, must be fulfilled, and the like. He manifestly accepted the old dispensation as a sacred and divine communication which could not, in principle or in essential and important fact, be broken. And we cannot conceive Him to have been wrong here without striking at the root of His claims upon our reverence as the Son of God, because it was no mere error of opinion that was involved, but an entire misrepresentation of His position and of His relation to Scripture in virtue of it. But it is impossible that Scripture, as Scripture, should have had this significance with regard to Him, and not have been possessed of characteristics altogether unlike those of any human composition. If the Old Testament did point to Christ, and in whatever sense it did, it must have been endowed with supernatural features and qualifications. And so far as it was so endowed, it may justly be regarded as the Word of God. But yet, forasmuch as not every word or sentence of the Old Testament could be so strained as to refer to Christ, or was even alleged to refer to Him, it is clear that this characteristic of the Old Testament was one affecting it as an organic whole, rather than attaching to its individual parts. We dare not say, however, that those passages only that are directly applied to Christ were the Word of God, because they were an integral portion of the whole, and could by no means be severed from the whole. That they were what they were tended rather to elevate the character of the whole to which they belonged, and by no means warranted us in limiting to them the reverence and respect with which they were justly regarded. On the contrary, if they were precious because Divine, so also might the documents containing them be regarded as Divine, because of the preciousness of what they contained. Just as the body of a living man is instinct with life in its several parts, although every part is not vital, so may Holy Scripture, or rather, for the present, the Old Testament, be regarded as instinct with the spirit of God as a whole, although it is only in certain parts that we can detect the spirit as more especially present, because of its supernatural testimony to Christ. And yet we may rightly say that it is the organic whole that is inspired, and not merely the individual parts. For instance, to take the Psalms: we know that our Lord regarded parts of the Psalms as distinctly referring to Him. And yet it was the Psalms as a whole, and not merely those parts of the Psalms, that we must regard as "inspired," and as "the Word of God;" for there is every reason to believe that many parts of the Psalms not cited by Christ, referred to Him not less than those which He quotes. It was the dignity put upon the Psalms as the vehicle of the Divine Spirit which made them the depository of those passages, and it was not the passages themselves that made the Psalms other than they were by nature, namely, the vehicle of the Divine Spirit. They were the compositions of men specially endowed with the Spirit of God for a particular purpose, and it was the fact that God spake by these men that made their writings so precious, and not merely the fact that they happened to give utterance to certain things which, left to themselves, they would have been unable to utter.

We are brought, then, to this conclusion : that it is the organic unity of the Old Testament and its main divisions that constitutes its characteristic feature, and not the fact that it contains certain sayings and utterances of exceptional and unique value. It is of course obvious that not all parts of the Old Testament, any more than all parts of any other book, are of equal value. The genealogical and numerical lists of Chronicles, Ezra, and Nehemiah, and the prescriptions of the Levitical ordinances, cannot be ranked intrinsically so high as the prophecies of Isaiah, nor could any man in his senses venture to rank them so; but for all that, forasmuch as these, equally with those, are intrinsic parts of an organic whole, and have their place, which cannot be dispensed with, in an organic whole, therefore, if the organic whole is entitled to be regarded as the Word of God, then are these parts portions also of that Word, and then we are not warranted in saying that the Old Testament contains the Word of God, if by so saying we mean to correct and confute the statement that the Old Testament is the Word of God. For to say this would be to deny the organic unity of that which is a whole in itself, and which, as a whole in itself, is possessed of the characteristics which make it the vehicle of that agency by virtue of which its more remarkable features are what they are. To sever these from the whole, and to limit the Divine agency of inspiration to them, would be to do violence to the book which it could not survive as a whole, and which would be equally fatal to its most characteristic parts.

But then arises the difficult question, what makes the Old Testament or the New an organic whole? What right have we to assume that either of them is an organic whole, capable of being thus differentiated from all other writings? And here, setting aside the question of canonicity, which has succeeded in including certain books within its charmed circle and excluding others, it may be observed that we can hardly avoid ascribing a certain unity in the first place to certain portions, and then finally to the whole, whether that whole is defined by canonicity or not. For instance, to take the Book of Genesis. That book, as we have it, is a recognisable whole in itself, however much criticism may persist in disintegrating it. After all, the Book of Genesis is the Book of Genesis, and there is a substantial unity pervading it whereby the several parts hang together and form a whole, however earnestly we or others may insist upon their original independence. Now it is this actual and essential unity with which we have to deal. The Book of Genesis contains several passages of the highest importance individually; these passages are not confined to any one separate portion of the whole, but are characteristic of the book generally. They are found in the third chapter, the twenty-second chapter, the forty-ninth chapter, and elsewhere.

These passages, then, are characteristic of the Book of Genesis as an organic whole, because they are not confined to one or other of its component parts. They are features characteristic of the essential unity of the book as we have it. They serve to mark the typical standard of the whole. The book is what they are. Because they are what they are, the book, as a whole, is what it is. No one would think of dragging down the estimate of the book to the value of its genealogical details, for example, or the like. The value of the book, as a whole, is determined by the value of its most important parts; it is they which stamp the whole as a whole. I do not mean that they show the book to be a whole, but that they show it as a whole to be what it is. In like manner the Book of Genesis itself is an integral portion of the Pentateuch.

The Pentateuch, as a whole, is to be estimated by the value of Genesis and Deuteronomy, for example, and what they are it is, not in all parts, but as a whole. Nobody proposes to add any other books or portions to the Pentateuch; but the Pentateuch, as we have it, is the Pentateuch, and rightly or wrongly, Genesis and Deuteronomy are characteristic portions of it, apart altogether from any points dependent upon questions of criticism. In like manner, what is true of Genesis and Deuteronomy with regard to the Pentateuch, is true of the Pentateuch itself with regard to the rest of the Old Testament.

The Old Testament is the Old Testament, whether or not we include in it the books that do not exist in the Hebrew. These books may not be canonical, but even if they are added to the Old Testament, seeing that nobody proposes to add any others, the question of their canonicity does not hinder us from regarding the Old Testament, and justly regarding it, as a whole. And thus the Old Testament, as a whole, must be estimated by the intrinsic value of its most important parts, and on the unique character and importance of them may rightly be differentiated from all other compositions which are wanting in these special characteristics.

We are now in a position to appreciate the kind

of authority that the New Testament assigns to the Old, when it speaks of it as Scripture. For as it is certain that these writings are possessed of features which are found nowhere else, so it is certain that the writers of the New Testament referred to the books in this capacity and regarded them as Scripture, or the written Word of God; that is to say, not as books which merely contained the Word of God, which they undoubtedly did, but as books which were, in their unique history, growth, composition, and the like, the providentially formed vehicle and chosen embodiment of that Word, so that God committed to them as a whole, whether we make that whole greater or less, the communication of His will to man.

The analogy of the human body seems to be one that we may again apply here, inasmuch as the feeble members are members still, and honourable from their connection with the body, although not every member can receive the light of day or give utterance to the more immediate messages of the word and mind of God, or is employed to do so. In like manner, when we come to the New Testament, manifestly the words of Christ, if genuine, must have the highest claim on our reverence and regard; while the question, whether or not they are genuine, is one that lies altogether outside our present consideration, being practically involved in the fact of the New Testament, which is the subject of our discussion, being the New Testament. If we have not got a substantially accurate representation of the words of Christ, but merely the report of men who may or may not have been His disciples, then there is an end to the whole matter. The question rather is, assuming the genuineness of the New Testament as a whole, in what sense and within what limits is it the Word of God? And here, as before, if Christ is what He is represented as being, His own words must be of the very highest authority. They may surely be regarded, not as containing, but as being the Word of God. While with regard to the framework in which they are set, namely, the disciples' own narrative, that must surely borrow its authority not only from what it contains, but also from the fact of its being the vehicle presumably chosen and ordained to convey it. And here, in this case, the question of canonicity assumes a somewhat different aspect in relation to our inquiries, inasmuch as we are more concerned to know whether our received books are genuine, than we are to determine whether or not any others may be added to them. The character of the Old Testament as a whole is not greatly affected, whether or not it includes Wisdom, or Ecclesiasticus, or even Tobit; but the character of the New Testament as a whole is very seriously affected if we allow the Apocryphal gospels to be added to it. And, as a matter of fact, they never have formed part of it. Consequently the vital question is, whether the New Testament as it is is genuine; and this question lies, as I have said, rather beyond our present inquiry, inasmuch as we want to know the amount of authority we must assign to our existing books, assuming them to be genuine, rather than whether or not they are so; because if they are not genuine, then the whole discussion is foreclosed and is rendered useless.

In what sense, and within what limits, are the Acts of the Apostles, for instance, and the Epistles of St. Paul the Word of God? With regard to the Acts of the Apostles thus much is clear, that since the period covered by the history is on all grounds a most important one, the value of the record must be in proportion to the authenticity of the narrative, and assuming *this*, it follows naturally, if not necessarily, that the writer of it was delegated and commissioned to write hardly less directly than those who committed the gospel narrative to writing. And thus it is, at all events, significant that the ostensible author of this narrative was also apparently the writer of the third Gospel. It is therefore reasonable to suppose that he wrote with the highest possible sanction; while he tells us himself, in the preface to the Gospel, in words which must apply equally to the second treatise, that he had the best information that could be procured. If, therefore, these things were so, it is not hard to see that the Acts of the Apostles may well be a treatise which not only contains, but even is the Word of God, so far as the authority of its record is concerned; while that it contains that Word is no less clear, if we accept the mission and authority of the principal actors in the narrative, who ostensibly spoke and acted with a Divine commission to act and speak.

And with regard to the Epistles of St. Paul, it seems to be one of the ulterior purposes of the Acts of the Apostles to give the voucher and credentials of him who was destined to play so prominent a part in the foundation and extension of the Christian Church. From the fact that he had been a bitter foe and a strenuous persecutor, his message was liable at the first to be received with suspicion, and clearly was so received. It needed not only the generous intervention and testimony of Barnabas to the early Church, but also and no less the testimony of one like St.

Luke, whose praise was in the Gospel, to make that message intelligible and trustworthy to the Church of all time. And this is exactly what we have in the narrative of St. Luke on behalf of St. Paul, to prepare us for the acceptance and recognition of his writings as authoritative documents.

But when we have so accepted them, in what sense and within what limits can they be regarded as the Word of God? Now it so happens that one of the very earliest of those documents has a statement in it which bears upon this question, and if this statement is received as authoritative, it may serve to indicate the kind of deference with which we may accept the Pauline epistles generally. St. Paul refers to his own oral preaching, and says that when the Thessalonians heard it they received it not as the word of men, but, as it really was, the Word of God, " which effectually worketh also in you that believe." Here, therefore, there are certain points which stand out with sufficient clearness. First, the unrecorded and oral testimony is declared to have been the Word of God. It did not merely contain, but it was the Word of God. This is the more remarkable, because it is impossible for us to determine definitely what was the nature of this communication. We know, indeed, within certain limits and from analogy, what was its subject matter, but we can form no idea as to its precise form or substance. We are therefore warranted in concluding that it was the subject matter of the communication, and not the particular form in which it was cast, that made it the Word of God. The form was altogether subordinate to the subject matter. The subject matter of the communication, and the authority with which it was proclaimed, made it to be the Word of God. And the vouchers for the authority of it are to be found in the declarations of St. Paul himself, and in what is told us confirmatory of those declarations by the writer of the Acts of the Apostles.

Given the truth of the solemn declarations of St. Paul himself, the authenticity of the events relating to his history, and the unique character of his position, and we must have every reason to accept his communications, as the Thessalonians did, not as the word of man, but as in very truth the Word of God. To question the authority of his word would be to question the authority of his office and mission, and to question the authority of his office and mission would be to throw discredit on the mere historical value of the Christian records, which we cannot do without sapping the foundations of the Christian faith itself. Thus the authority of a very large portion of the New Testament, as the special organ and channel of Divine communication, is secured to us by the admission of its simply historical character and authority. If the documents are in any true sense what they profess to be, it is evident and obvious that we must have in them documents of unique importance and of the very highest authority,—documents which must not only contain the Word of God, but must also be the authorised expression and embodiment of that Word, as no other writings can be.

It would seem, then, that we are gradually arriving at some distinct and definite answer to the question—In what sense is the Bible the Word of God? It is so in the sense that it may be presumed to have the Divine sanction and authentication as no other book has or can have. If the origin and claims of the Bible are what they are, then it has a just right to be regarded as a communication to man charged with Divine authority. The Old Testament is shown to be so, because of the distinct and otherwise inexplicable witness that it bears to Christ; and the New Testament is shown to be so because it cannot be otherwise, unless its documents are actual forgeries and impostures, as they most certainly are not. The Bible, then, is the Word of God *because it is the authorised record of the way in which God communicated His will to man, and because it is the appointed instrument for making known that will.* And the proof that it is this lies in the credentials that it is able to bring with it, to which there is nothing analogous elsewhere in literature; and also in the effect with which its due reception is followed, which is likewise indicated in those other words of St. Paul: "which effectually worketh also in you that believe," from which we learn two facts of great and primary importance; first, that it is characteristic of the Word of God to be *fruitful*,—"It shall not return unto Me void, but shall accomplish that which I please, and shall prosper in the thing whereto I sent it;" and secondly, that this fruitfulness is conditioned by and dependent upon the *faith* of the recipient of the message. It is of the greatest consequence to note this contingency, because it shows us plainly, if it is a true contingency, as it cannot fail to be, that whether or not this that we have is the Word of God, it would not be possible to have any Word of God that would not be liable to be rejected, and to become unfruitful, where there was not the requisite measure of faith in the recipient. A moment's consideration will show that it must be so if the Divine message is to be conveyed upon probable and not upon demonstrative evidence. Because in that case it must appeal to the moral faculties, to educate which may be presumed to be one of the immediate objects of the Divine communication. The supposed Word of God comes to us seeking acceptance among those who are like-minded with itself. To them it offers points of attraction which are lacking in the case of others, and antecedently there is nothing improbable in a revelation, if made, being accepted by some and rejected by others, unless it were so given as to *compel* acceptance; and if this was not the case, those who accepted it would have qualifications which others would lack, and among these would necessarily be the qualification and faculty of *faith*. "In you that believe;" therefore, while it effectually limits the area of acceptance, presents no condition that could not be antecedently perceived to be inevitable in the case of any presumed revelation coming from God, and appealing to the judgment of man. Under all imaginable conditions faith would be an indispensable requisite, unless man were to be deprived of his essential prerogative of free choice. While, then, the efficacy of the Word of God is confined to those who receive it believingly, among all faithful recipients it is the characteristic of that Word to be operative and fruitful, so much so that this is the one token of the Word of God which the Apostle selects, and which, in fact, differentiates it from every other *word*.

The Word of God is proved to be the Word of God, not only by the validity of its credentials, but by the power with which it works, as nothing else can work, upon the believing heart; and the sense in which the Bible is the Word of God is in the fulness and sufficiency of authority with which it comes to us, as the means specially ordained by God for making known His will to us. In this sense the Bible is the Word of God, as no other book of never so high a moral tone and purpose can pretend to be. God has spoken by and in this book as He has spoken by and in no other. For in no other book is there the evidence of His presiding Spirit and influence that there is in the composition and contents of this book. If otherwise, let the book which can rival this be at once named and tested on its merits, when it will forthwith appear that, whether or not the credentials of this book are satisfactory, those of any other are altogether wanting.

We must turn now to the investigation of the second question: within what limits is the Bible the Word of God? That is to say, given the inspiration and authority of the Bible as a fact, how is the character of the Bible influenced and affected thereby? And in this respect the truth would seem to lie between two extremes. First, the action of any mechanical inspiration must be rejected. The Bible is not the Word of God in any such sense, as that every word and letter that occurs in it is thereby made to be something which it would not be if it occurred elsewhere. Every word and letter of the Bible is not God's Word because it is found in the Bible, and as it is there found. The truth of analogy holds good in the Bible as it does elsewhere. Thus the Puritanical use of the Bible as a storehouse of words deliberately arranged so as to form a rigid and metallic standard for the regulation at haphazard of every conceivable circumstance in life, is superstitious in the highest degree, and unworthy of the free agency and wisdom of the Spirit of God. That there may historically be some remarkable instances in which direction has been sought and found in this way, by no means warrants the inference that this is the right and ideal use of the Bible, or that it is intended to be so used. The story is told of Simeon, that when he was feeling the burden of opposition and contempt more than usual, he found remarkable support in accidentally lighting on the passage, "They compelled one Simon, a Cyrenian, to bear His cross," because he remembered that Simon and Simeon were the same name. It is needless to say that such a method of using Scripture is childish in the extreme, and most derogatory to the wisdom and freedom of the Holy Spirit. Here, then, in this superstitious estimate of the words of Scripture we may surely discover one limit *within* which it may be defined as the Word of God. It is not the Word of God in any such sense or for any such purpose as this; we should do it great dishonour if we thought so. The book of God is not different from any other book in the laws of its composition, the changes and chances of its tradition, its liability to errors of transcription, its dependence upon the watchfulness of its human guardians, and the like. But just as all these contingencies do not prevent us from possessing, and highly prizing the possession of, a Shakespeare, Virgil, or Thucydides, so neither do they take from us the priceless treasure of which God has given us the possession in His Word; nor do they prevent the Bible from being His Word in a sense in which these books, and all others like them, can make no pretension to being. This then is one extreme within which the truth must lie; another is of an opposite kind. If the Bible is the Word of God at all, it must be so in such a sense as that we may trust its most important and crucial utterances to the very letter. Supposing the exact words to have been accurately ascertained, there seems to be no limit to which we may not trust and rely upon them to the very letter. If words are the vehicles of thought, then the more exact the thought the more accurate the words must be, unless they are to misrepresent and not do justice to it. And there are ten thousand instances in which the Word of God is thus the Word of God, or it must fail altogether as a trustworthy record of His will. In all human compositions the value of the thing written depends upon the truth and faithfulness with which it reflects the mind of the writer. Can it be otherwise with the Divine writings? If we cannot trust their *ipsissima verba* when we most stand in need of learning the Divine will, what is there that we can trust? Nay, is it not reasonable to suppose that if we have any such word at all in the Bible, then there must be vast treasures of wealth still unexplored in it, rich veins of virgin ore which are waiting to reveal and render up their secrets to the faith and patience of the student, and the favouring opportunities of some fresh emergency? We find it was with no niggard spirit of verbal reliance that the writers of the New Testament appealed to the writings of the Old, and even if in some cases it may be hard for us to accept their conclusions with the fulness of entire consent, we may at least assume that their practice has set us an example which we shall not do wrong in following, and established a principle which may be a certain guide to us in our estimate of the character of the Divine Word. Here, then, we discover the traces of a limit on the other side, within which the truth must lie. We must have so accurate a verbal transcript of the will of God that we may be able to depend upon it for teaching us His will; but, on the other hand, we must beware of making such a use of the Divine words that they cease to be the intelligent exponents of the Divine counsels, and become only the slaves of an unintelligent and random destiny. The Psalmist believed that there were treasures in the Divine word which he might discover, or might fail to perceive, and therefore prayed, "Open Thou mine eyes, that I may see the wondrous things of Thy law;" while at the same time he recognised the fact that it was a vast repository of *principle,* for permanent and inexhaustible application in the affairs of life, when he said, "The righteousness of Thy testimonies is everlasting: O grant me understanding and I shall live."

Within these limits, then, it would seem that we shall be warranted in regarding the Bible as the Word of God. We shall not do justice to it if we pervert it to an occasion of superstitious use. We shall most assuredly fail to recognise its just claims if we suppose that it cannot teach us, as no other book has the authority to do, the mind and will of God, and that it cannot make its every word and select expression the vehicle of imparting the knowledge of that will, when it is expedient and desirable that we should know it. "Seek, and ye shall find," has its application here no less than elsewhere, and the necessary inference is, that if we do not seek we shall not find; though it is no less true that it will be utterly useless for us to seek unless there is that in the Book, though hidden from the common view, which will most richly and bountifully reward the patient, faithful, and laborious search.

Article III.

By the Rev. Principal JOHN CAIRNS, D.D.

IN following up the able paper of Professor Stanley Leathes on this question, I have, for a writer, the disadvantage of agreeing too closely with his point of view. This will hardly keep the discussion going: only your next contributor (if you have such), who takes what he regards as a freer position, may find more materials for reply in two statements than in one. I am glad to be in harmony with Dr. Leathes, all the more that the tide has, perhaps, for some time run the other way. I have lived through a great deal of modification on the Inspiration question on the part of men otherwise evangelical; while I do not find that my own views have changed. The Bible is to me, in all its parts, a more Divine book than ever it was. I am not able to answer a good many difficulties which beset a strict theory of Inspiration; but it seems, as of old, the best supported by evidence and the one likely to keep the field.

I shall not, perhaps, adhere very closely to the

distinction taken in the question between *the sense in which*, and the *limits within which*, the Bible may be regarded as the Word of God. I wish to begin with a few negatives which belong to both positions. In setting aside what we do not need to hold, when saying that the Bible is the Word of God, we so far clear the field on both sides.

I. *First*, then, We do not need to hold that the question of the canon has been fully settled. I, for one, have no quarrel with that settlement; but though I might not see my way to accept the Book of Esther or the Second Epistle of Peter, if I held a Word of God, I might equally hold that Word all inspired and in the highest sense. As Professor Stanley Leathes has said, the questions are distinct; though, of course, if no canon were left, this question also of the nature and degree of inspiration would fall.

II. *Secondly*, We do not need to hold that the present text is the very Word of God. This remark is a mere extension of the foregoing. The change from the original MSS. to the best extant critical text is so far a sacrifice of canonicity. But we know how little really this means, and how it is always becoming less. The calmness with which even the ordinary mind has taken all the discussion connected with the Revised New Testament, is creditable to public intelligence. We see that, to all intents and purposes, the Word of God has not been lost in transcription, so that while we must draw the distinction, it is not a grave one, between the Bible as we have it, and as it first came from God.

III. We do not, *thirdly*, need to hold that the Bible is all, as to the matter of it, revealed for the first time. No one can ever have held this, even when less freedom prevailed as to the question of inspiration than now. Moses could not be informed, for the first time, of the events which he himself had witnessed; nor Luke of the incidents of Paul's shipwreck. Innumerable historical monuments existed, such as the decrees of Cyrus and Darius as to the re-building of the Temple, the registers of the Davidic family and others, the letter of the Council of Jerusalem to the Gentile Christians, and other documents. Nor can this be limited to historical matter. To suppose that the matter of the Psalms of David was all as new to him as the revelation that the Messiah was to spring from his line, is what no one can maintain; or that Solomon had never conceived anything like any of his Proverbs; or that Paul, who had taught it in the synagogue at Antioch years before, had the doctrine of Justification revealed to him when he was about to write the Epistles to the Galatians and to the Romans. Much of the Bible was, no doubt, revealed to the writers, partly at the time when they wrote, as in the visions of the Prophets and of the Apocalypse; and partly long before, as in the earlier training of the Apostles, for we see how Paul repeatedly claims this privilege. But beyond all question a very large part of the Bible pre-existed, without any proper revelation, in the materials out of which it was made. The revelation in regard to them consisted of the use that was to be made of them, and in the Divine workmanship that formed them into a new and higher whole.

IV. We do not, *fourthly*, need to hold that the Bible, as to the manner of it, is in such a sense the Word of God, as not also to be the word of man. In recent times much more light has been cast upon what has been called the human element in the Bible; and this has been unwelcome to some because it has not unfrequently tended, if not to exclude, yet to lower, the Divine. This, however, has been an abuse and not a just use of a great and important principle in theological science. The Bible expressly recognises this human element in itself. "Which things," says Paul, "*we* speak."

"We also believe, and therefore speak." These assertions are made in connection with the strongest claims to Divine inspiration. It is to my mind, one of the internal evidences of the canonicity of Second Peter, that it so clearly brings out the two sides in inspired teaching: "Holy men of God spake as they were moved by the Holy Ghost." "Even as our beloved brother Paul also, according to the wisdom given unto him, hath written unto you." Our Lord recognises the 110th Psalm as David's, in a true sense, "How then doth David in spirit call him Lord?" and remarkable is the introduction of the personality of David into the matter by Peter on the day of Pentecost, "For David is not ascended into the heavens, but he saith himself (αὐτός) The Lord said unto *my* Lord," &c. Many similar references could be produced; and the effect of all is to establish a genuine authorship for those who were the writers of the sacred books. I, therefore, accept the recommendation of the American Committee, that the word "by" should be uniformly "through;" for it is more than a question of philology, viz.: as I understand it, a question of doctrine, and of this doctrine of real human authorship, that is involved. This differentiates the Word of God from all other professed revelations. Thus, in the Koran, Mahomet is purely passive and recipient. Everything is spoken in one long monotonous utterance, as by the direct voice of God. Now, in the Bible, no doubt, there are considerable portions here and there, as in the writings of the prophets, where this style seems to be used. But I cannot agree with those who think that anywhere there is such a suppression of the human element as, in other religions, is the ideal form of revelation. In the sublimest utterances of prophecy there is an assimilation of style to the individuality of the prophet, and as no one will suppose that this was a mere external adaptation, these oracles must have gone through the souls of the prophets and taken a colour from the human medium thus passed through. It is very difficult, if not impossible, for us to understand the psychology of this subject, but the facts are indubitable: and the more closely the literature of the Bible is studied, the more profound does this impression become. The only exception, perhaps, is in the Decalogue, which is said to have come in a way altogether *sui generis:* though the variations in Deuteronomy show the human element even here. The words of our Lord are no exception; for He was the "Son of Man;" and, besides, we see in the Johannine reflection of them another human peculiarity. So far from weakening the interest of the Bible, this law greatly, and in comparison with other professed revelations, unspeakably enhances it. It will not be questioned that if God can speak through fifty human voices, all different, the attraction and impression are greater than if He speaks merely by one. This, of course, implies that in all these human voices the one Divine voice, sounding through them and above them, is recognisable. This, it is contended, is the fact; and hence the doctrine of a true human individuality and authorship in the Bible, so far from being, as is sometimes objected, a lowering of the miracle of inspiration, is, if possible, an elevation of it. A more rigid and metallic style of inspiration, if I may so express myself, while beyond all question less human, would also have been less Divine, than the infinitely varied and flexible, and in every sense unparalleled, organ which we have. It could not have helped being literature, in every form consistent with its own grandeur and seriousness. But it would not have stood at the head of the literature of the world, an external monument between earth and heaven.

Having made these distinctions, which clear our way, we are now, I think, prepared for answering better the *two* questions. In what sense, and within what limits, the Bible may be regarded as the Word of God? Very little needs to be said as to *the sense* in which the Bible is the Word of God. It must either mean that the Bible has in it matter which, simply on the ground of its being true and naturally discernible, comes from God. Or it must mean that it comes by a supernatural communication or revelation. This is the great battle-field between the Rationalist and the Believer; but, as Professor Stanley Leathes has shown, it does not need to be occupied long for our purpose. Whoever holds a special Divine message in the Bible— beyond the mere outgrowth of human intelligence —if he only speaks of the Bible as *containing* the Word of God, and knows what he means, has conceded a sense to the Bible quite unlike what belongs to any other book. It has, no doubt, a human author or authors; but God is its true, its deepest author. It comes from God. It only could come from God, and thus it is the Word of God. *Further*, as being from God, the Bible necessarily manifests Divine properties, intelligence, wisdom, holiness, tenderness, all more or less recognisable, and thus, by their presence and evidence, is also the Word of God. But, to *crown all*, the Bible speaks with Divine authority to those who are God's creatures and subjects; and thus being not only an utterance but a command, it is the Word of God. The Bible is not only a royal letter, but a royal proclamation. It makes not only mind, but will, known; it may be in a thousand ways of indirect and gentle, as well as more summary and abrupt authority; and its highest strain seems even to forget that the creature is the medium, as well as the subject, of revelation. "Thus saith the Lord." "Hear ye the Word of the Lord." Now, I think that Professor Stanley Leathes has here found a right starting-point for the *limits* of inspiration in its very *nature*, for whatever can be connected and bound up with this admitted, undeniable, transcendent element, where the presence of the Word of God shines in its own light, must necessarily share the privilege. His thesis, I think, is this, that the argument for *any* Bible leads also to a *full* Bible. Let us simply go over his applications of this principle, and see if there are any others.

He founds on the *organic unity* of the Bible, instancing in particular, Genesis, the Pentateuch, the Gospels, and extending the argument from all the parts to the whole. Now this is just what I have said, the extension of Divinity in a part to

Divinity in the whole. The details then lie, after the general principle is accepted, in settling the actual organic unity. This can only be by general Christian consent, or even general literary consent. Non-canonicity, interpolation, or similar difficulties, would here be the only demurrers to this plea. It could hardly be checked by a denial of the principle, that inspiration *anywhere* does, in the nature of things, cover it *everywhere*, so far as organic unity in a communication extends.

This also applies to another argument of Professor Stanley Leathes, *the testimony of our Lord in dealing with the Old Testament.* It is presupposed that His part of the recorded communication shines in its own light as Divine, and also that we have His words with sufficient accuracy to reason from them. It is hardly necessary to meet the difficulties of those who allow that our Lord, in His humbled state, might be voluntarily ignorant of the number and value of sacred books. The argument, then, that is drawn from our Lord's references, not only to the canonicity of the Old Testament, but to the complete inspiration of its several parts, as resting on His quotations, His appeals, His absolute deference to the Old Testament record, seems impossible to set aside; but it is just the extension of revelation from one point to another, from our Lord as the Divine centre, to the circumference of the system.

Another consideration pressed is *the claim made by the sacred writers.* In so far as they appeal to each other, with entire deference, whether in the Old Testament Scriptures or in the New, this is only the same argument with the testimony of our Lord. But in so far as they claim peculiar light and authority for themselves as writers, the argument is distinct. In some sense, it even comes closer than that of Christ Himself; since He delivers no writing of His own, casting over every part of it the same claim to authority. It cannot fairly be denied that these claims are great and singular. Thus Paul: "If any man think himself to be a prophet or spiritual, let him acknowledge that the things that I write unto you are the commandments of the Lord." And thus also John: "We are of God: he that knoweth God heareth us; he that is not of God heareth not us; hereby know we the spirit of truth and the spirit of error." Here again is the application of the same principle, the extension from the part to the whole, with the same visible cogency of sequence: for if such claims break down in professed teachers at any point, there is delusion and miscarriage. It is indeed possible that an agent of revelation may distinguish, in a message, a part which he excludes from his general divinely guaranteed utterance. Some, as is well known, think this the case with the Apostle Paul in 1 Cor. vii. But this is hardly the general view; and if it were so, the exception would prove the rule.

The only other topic, as far as I have noticed, adduced by Professor Stanley Leathes to settle the limits of the Word of God is *its success*. This, again, would be an argument from what is Divine at one point to what is Divine all through. If Divine influence, in a book itself, or coming from without, work in a transcendent way, the whole vehicle is exalted. This argument also must be held, in the circumstances, to be sound. No doubt Divine Providence may work, and work great things, by imperfect instruments. But hardly by a book which denies, or conceals, its own imperfection, which exaggerates its nearness to heaven, and goes through the world with a general title to infallibility, deserving to be rebuked and discredited.

It now remains to see whether any farther applications of the same principle may be found, beyond those rapidly enumerated. One may be suggested, viz., the appeal of our Lord to the authority of the Old Testament, *as admitting of extension to the New.* Our Lord, of course, could not ratify the New Testament; but He could anticipate it, He could provide for it, and use words which fairly cover its contents. Hence the great body of interpreters have applied His words as to the Spirit leading into all truth, and assisting His witnesses when brought before kings and magistrates, as fairly including the writing of the New Testament histories and epistles. It would be quite anomalous to have divinely provided records of Old Testament revelation vouched for by the Saviour, while the last, and, in many respects, greatest stage of revelation remained without supply or guarantee. This is not a mere *à priori* deduction. The strongest evidence of fact would be needed to show that, for some mysterious reason, the analogy did not hold. Hence the Church will never believe that documents which seem to meet this want did not mean to do so, or that New Testament Scripture was less carefully produced and less minutely superintended, than that which our Lord treated with such unquestioning submission.

Another application, founded on the same principle of extension, is that *from the prophecies of the Bible.* A book thus exalted becomes everywhere sacred. I believe that a true argument could be founded also on miracles. I do not share the distrust of miracles as seals of revelation, and of all that the miracle worker may be fairly held to bind up with God's name. But in the case of prophecy, the extension from part to whole is immediate, since prophecy, unlike miracles, is itself part of a book. What, then, is to bar the extension, or bring down the revealer of the future, whatever be his theme, from the highest authority? The reverence of the Jews for the prophets was thus most rational. Nor will the case of bad prophets, or of injudicious gifted men, bar the inference. A bad man like Balaam was not allowed to trade with his gift; nor were the gifted Corinthians, as far as we see, allowed to teach false doctrine. This conclusion carries us a long way to a universal Word of God, for prophecy, like a golden thread, runs all through from Genesis to Revelation.

I will only add that *parts of Scripture, almost as wonderful as prophecies, rising at different points all through the organism of the Bible*, maintain the sense of its unbroken divinity. This is not quite the same thing with the organic unity already considered. That would be the same, though the higher organs were all in one region; but here, so to speak, they are distributed throughout the body. The master-pieces of the Bible, narrative, moral, doctrinal, lyrical, are never far off from each other. It cannot be held that the main parts are finished with such incomparable skill, and the minor neglected. When we see how the Mosaic, Davidic, Solomonic, Pre-exilic and Post-exilic books have each their great features, and yet all foreshadow Christ and the New Testament; and how again the histories of Christ, so unique, grow into the Acts, pass into the Epistles, and culminate in the Apocalypse, which sums up history, doctrine, prophecy and devotion in one, it is not possible to hold a partial theory of the inspiration of Scripture. "Deep calleth unto deep." It is "as the voice of many waters," and "as the voices of harpers harping with their harps."

It only remains, in closing this paper, to touch in the briefest way upon a few objections and difficulties. Those of a scientific kind may be almost passed over. It is now universally admitted that the Bible was not given to teach science, and could not even have taught it, had it been desired. Nor is cosmogony science, but something which precedes it; so that science never can properly criticise a cosmogony, and a moral and popular statement of a cosmogony, which antecedes its own career. So of the deluge; if it be a miracle, to bring it, like Reimarus, to natural law, is, as Lessing said, to destroy it.

Ethical difficulties are now much less urged than formerly. They chiefly belong to the region of the Old Testament; and they may be largely covered, though doubtless some remain, by the principle that the Mosaic system was confessedly imperfect, and that evils remained in it—not yet curable—"through the hardness of the people's hearts." Besides, it needs, in some cases, discrimination to see what is simply reported, and what is approved. Doctrinal difficulties and contradictions are also abated in their pressure. Such alleged discords, as between James and Paul, have failed to wound; and while variation of type is more conceded in our Biblical Theology, this is not generally allowed to be more than the different side of truth. It is indeed remarkable how rarely, even in rationalistic schools, the Apostle Paul is now charged with arbitrary or inconclusive reasoning. The chief field of difficulty in regard to the full integrity of the Word of God, is the historical —and that with a large and growing admission of historical accuracy. The discoveries in Egypt, Nineveh and Babylon, have assisted this result in the Old Testament; the failure of the mythical theory, and the growing acceptance of the Gospel data in the New. There are, no doubt, many problems, of which the harmonistic of the four Gospels can only give a conjectural solution. But this is really the case with all true history, especially as the historians are multiplied; and as, according to every reasonable theory of the human element in inspiration, the Spirit of God did not shed over the mind of each sacred writer all the illumination that the rest possessed, but wrought, without being limited to this, with his pre-existing mass of knowledge, moulding it to higher ends, so the results seem to vary, because, in the absence of an anxious and studied harmony, the links of reconciliation are not supplied. But any one who looks upon the four Gospels in their wonderful features, spiritual and literary, and on their not less wonderful effects, will, with reason, regard the evidence of their inspiration as not at all shaken by the remaining historical difficulties; will perhaps rather wonder that they are so few, and will adjourn them to a future, which is always learning better to cure or to endure them.

I may be permitted to close this paper with a few sentences from the speech of Bishop Temple at the late meeting of the Bible Society, in which many will hail, if not a change, a happy clearing up of misunderstanding, and a welcome omen of

British thought. "I have read the writings of good men and of great men; I have read the writings of great philosophers of old—of men who saw far deeper into the truth, by the power of wonderful intellects, guided no doubt by God's providence, than it was possible for ordinary men to see. I have read many books which set before the soul the loftiest motives of action, and the most heavenly principles to guide the conduct. And still, wherever we turn, as we read them all we feel that they are referred to our own consciences to judge; that we still are called to discriminate, and to say, 'Here I accept, and there I reject;' and though a man be a greater man than I, still my judgment remains responsible for its own decision, and I cannot shift the responsibility on any other shoulders than my own. And I have read many such books, and have felt that I learned much; and still, for all that, there remains the sense that these books, though they are my teachers, are not my rulers, and though they instruct me, they cannot command me. But when I turn to the Word of God, it takes me straight, as it were, into God's very presence, and gives its message thereby an authority which is His and His alone."

Article IV.

By the Rev. ALEX. MACKENNAL, M.A.

I HAVE read with interest the papers of Professor Stanley Leathes and Principal Cairns, and fully accord with them in their purpose of establishing for the Bible a unique place in literature, and in their affirmation that this is characteristic of the Bible as a whole, and not merely of some detached portions of it. I accept the statement of Dr. Leathes that the Bible is "the authorised record of the way in which God communicated His will to man, and [that] it is the appointed instrument for making known that will." I too should assert that the Bible is an organic whole, a Divine book; the life pulsates through every part. But these papers, in my judgment, completely fail in establishing their thesis that the Bible may properly be spoken of as the Word of God. For many years I have hesitated so to speak of it; and my hesitation is increased rather than abated by the arguments of Dr. Leathes and Dr. Cairns. In saying this I do not, as Dr. Cairns suggests, regard myself as taking a "freer position" than his; my complaint is that he is too "free" as an interpreter, that he goes counter to the analogy of Scripture, and disregards a distinction which the Bible writers carefully maintain.

That is a significant fact on which Professor Radford Thomson dwells, that "the Scriptures do not explicitly claim to be the Word of God, nor does any one of the books of which they are composed put forward this claim." He might have gone further and said that the Scriptures implicitly repudiate it. I wish to emphasise Mr. Warrington's statement, quoted by Mr. Thomson, that "the phrase in question occurs three or four hundred times in the Old Testament, and a hundred times in the New, but is never once applied to Scripture itself." The force of such statements is not to be weakened by the reminder that the whole Bible was not completed while its books were being written, and that until the "organic whole" was complete, its value could not be appraised. The very distinction, the propriety of which Dr. Leathes denies, between the Bible and some of its contents, is grounded on Scriptural usage. A peculiar consciousness in the person who was the medium of the Revelation is ever connoted when the phrase is used; the "Word of God" is God's direct communication; there are specially authoritative statements even of inspired men; especially urgent messages are given to the prophets, exalting their moods, compelling them to speak. The writers of the Bible are careful to mark these out; they do not confound them with the work of the historian, the scribe, the poet, even when they treat the writings of poet, scribe, historian with the reverence due to Holy Scripture.

In the Old Testament the phrase "the Word of the Lord" is freely applied to the Law; and this is perfectly intelligible. The whole history is so constructed as to give us the idea of an objective revelation, not in any wise to be confounded with the development of the religious consciousness, or the impulses and reasonings even of an inspired man. The place where the revelation is to be made—Sinai or the tabernacle of the congregation—is solemnly fenced off and consecrated; the face of Moses shines on his descent from the mountain; the cloud descends and covers him while the Lord is communicating His will. The lawgiver is distinguished from those who prophesy; there is to be no confusion between the distinct revelations imparted to him, and the imagery, needing to be interpreted and clothed in their own language, which God causes to pass before the minds of the prophets. "Hear now my words, If there be a prophet among you, I the Lord will make myself known unto him in a vision, and will speak unto him in a dream. My servant Moses is not so, who is faithful in all Mine house. With him will I speak mouth to mouth, even apparently, and not in dark speeches; and the similitude of the Lord shall he behold." Persons who believed such a narrative as that of Moses might well understand that the Law given through him was to be received as authoritative until its abolition should be announced in an equally impressive and unmistakable manner; to him it was the Word of the Lord. But it is to me inconceivable that they should apply—as a matter of fact they did not apply—the phrase whose solemn import was thus assured to them, to such stories as that of the apostasy under Sinai, or of even the intercession of the inspired saint for Miriam.

In the prophetical history we find the frequent iteration of the phrase, "The Word of God," or, "of the Lord." Here, too, it is always used of special revelations; the revelations are, however, not now of permanent, but of passing, personal, local, circumstantial application. The whole body of prophecy is not spoken of, *simpliciter*, as the Word of the Lord; the phrase used is the Word of the

Lord "which He spake by the hand of Ahijah the Shilonite to Jeroboam the son of Nebat;" "the Word of the Lord by the mouth of Jeremiah, until the land had enjoyed her Sabbaths;" and so on. A prophecy is only called the Word of God, or of the Lord, in relation to the circumstances which called it forth. It is contrary to Old Testament usage to generalise an utterance, to draw out its moral and spiritual significance into new applications, and call it in such applications "the Word of God." It is to me inconceivable that Jeremiah, for instance, who uses the phrase to express and vindicate the sense of solemn urgency under which he speaks, could have tolerated the application of it to the whole history in which his prophecies are enshrined, or even to his prophecies themselves as edited in a book.

Dr. Leathes says, that "the New Testament, beyond all question, claims and assumes that honour [the honour of being the Word of God] for the Old. We may take that for granted, and need not stop to prove it." This is an amazing statement; we can understand it only when we remember that it is of his own reading of the phrase "the Word of God" that Dr. Leathes is here speaking, not of the Scriptural usage. To me, fully accepting, as I do, what he says about the reverence paid in the New Testament to the Old, the significant fact is, that the phrase in question should not be employed. "The position assigned to the Old Testament by the New is very much that with which the Bible at large is regarded by religious people." I adopt the statement; and add, that "religious people" constantly speak of the Bible as the Word of God, but in the New Testament the Old Testament is never so styled. Dr. Cairns quotes as "one of the internal evidences of the canonicity of Second Peter, that it so clearly brings out the two sides in inspired teaching: 'holy men of God spake as they were moved by the Holy Ghost.'" Peter is here contrasting words spoken "by the will of man," and words spoken under the impulse of the Holy Ghost; and it would have been very natural for him to employ the phrase, "the Word of God," had it been the New Testament usage to apply that phrase to the Old Testament. The Apostle Paul does use this language when speaking to the Thessalonians of the authority of the gospel. "When ye received the Word of God which ye heard of us, ye received it not as the word of men, but as it is in truth, the Word of God, which effectually worketh also in you that believe." "The law," "the law and the prophets," "Moses and the prophets," "the law of

Moses, and the prophets and the Psalms," "the Scripture,"—these are all terms employed in the New Testament to designate the Old; and the idea of the sanctity and authority of these writings is sufficiently evident; but the New Testament writers do not, because of their regard for their sacred books, attach to them indiscriminately the title "Word of God." In the New Testament the phrase is commonly applied to the gospel as preached—"The grass withereth, and the flower thereof falleth away: but the Word of the Lord endureth for ever. And this is the Word which, by the gospel, is preached unto you;"—to the substance of the preaching of the apostles and evangelists—"They which were scattered abroad went everywhere preaching the Word;"—to the communication of the Father's will by Christ to the twelve—"I have given unto them Thy Word." This use of the term also is perfectly intelligible. The gospel was a direct and special revelation from God; it was *the* revelation, the unfolding of the mystery which prophets and wise men had waited for, and into which the angels had desired to look. The gospel was not, like the utterances of the prophets, merely of passing, personal, local, circumstantial application; it was not, like the law, given to a nation, intended to endure during the time of that nation's separation, and then to die away in a more excellent glory; it was for all ages and for all mankind, and so could be styled, *simpliciter*, "the Word." The restricted usage of the Old Testament had kept for New Testament times a term aptly expressive of the supreme and solitary claim of the gospel to be the perfect revelation of God's will to mankind; and after it had once been employed of the gospel, it could never be again used even in its Old Testament signification. For the reverence of men, trained in the Jewish habit of regarding the Word of God, as that which endureth for ever, could not have endured the application of the phrase to that which, in the language of the writer of the Epistle to the Hebrews, was decaying, and waxing old and ready to vanish away. Even the law now became "Scripture," and not "the Word of God." The Apostles were "ministers of the Word," and what is meant by this phrase the Apostle Paul tells us—" our sufficiency is of God, who also hath made us able ministers of the new [covenant] testament; not of the letter, but of the Spirit: for the letter killeth, but the Spirit giveth life. . . . Now the Lord is that Spirit: and where the Spirit of the Lord is, there is liberty."

This last quotation prepares us for John's loftiest

application of the term "Word," to the Lord Jesus Christ Himself. The only complete revelation of the Father is the Son; "No man knoweth the Father save the Son, and he to whomsoever the Son will reveal Him." That reservation of the term "the Word," to which I have alluded in the last paragraph, is seen to have this further significance. It first forbade the indiscriminate acceptance of the sayings of inspired men as utterances essentially Divine; it appeared in due time that special prophetic sayings, and even the law given by Moses, were only styled the Word of God in a partial and accommodative sense; it stamped a supreme and solitary grandeur on the gospel, and prepared us for the words spoken from heaven above the Christ—"This is my beloved Son: hear Him."

There is another significant difference between the use of the term "Word of the Lord" in the prophetic and in the New Testament histories. The Word of the Lord came to the prophets concerning personal matters, of small and trivial concern it might almost seem, as well as concerning great political and national events. The punishment of Shemaiah, for instance (Jer. xxix. 30-33), and the death of Ezekiel's wife, were announced as by "the Word of the Lord." In the apostolic history, such announcements are said to be by the Spirit, the Holy Ghost, not by the Word of the Lord. Paul was "forbidden of the Holy Ghost to preach the Word in Asia;" Agabus bound himself with Paul's girdle, and said, "Thus saith the Holy Ghost, So shall the Jews at Jerusalem bind the man that owneth this girdle, and shall deliver him into the hands of the Gentiles." Again we see restriction in the use of a very solemn phrase. It appears in the times of Moses; the Lord gave to the seventy elders (Num. xi.) "of the spirit that was upon" Moses; "Would God," says Moses, "that all the Lord's people were prophets, and that the Lord would put His spirit upon them." Their inspiration was not to be confounded with the speech of God to Moses, face to face; they did not receive and report the Word of God.

Fully to explain why the phrase might be employed as it was in the prophetic history would unduly prolong this paper. I would only suggest that the special revelations made to the prophets consisted frequently of a number of historical details; whereas in the times of Moses the law was the Revelation; and the gospel was so in the Apostolic period. I allude to the contrast in order to emphasize my point, that the distinction between the Word of God and the history in which it is communicated, between Revelation and Inspiration, is clearly marked in the Bible. The two great periods of special revelation, the times of Moses and of Christ, were also periods of widely diffused inspiration; and these are exactly the times when the peculiar significance of the phrase, " the Word of God," is most strictly guarded.

To sum up the affirmations of my paper—in the Old Testament, the term " Word of God" is applied only to special revelations, and to them only in relation to the circumstances under which the revelation was made : in the New Testament, which is the history of the foundation of a new dispensation, because the circumstances to which the law and special prophecies apply are, in God's purpose, completely changed, the term is no longer applied to them : the apostolic usage reserves the term to the revelation of God by His Son; the final employment of the term is the most exalted and restricted of all,—John's application of it to the personal Christ.

It may be said to me, "Granting that your exposition of the Biblical use of the phrase is substantially correct, is the ordinary Christian usage illegitimate? is it not pedantic to insist on the points on which you have been dwelling? would not the discontinuance of the common usage seem like yielding the authority of the Scriptures?" I reply, it cannot be pedantic, in deciding on the character of a book, to respect the representation it gives of itself; nor legitimate to disregard distinctions with which it supplies us for its interpretation. Both Dr. Leathes and Dr. Cairns are compelled, having regard to the present state of science, critical and otherwise, to lay down qualifications and make reserves which, to a Jew, would have seemed not very reverent treatment of the Word of God. The attempt to attach a name of special sanctity to all the contents of the Bible ends in the degradation of that name itself.

We understand what a man means when, urging some utterance on our attention, he says, "I give you my word for this;" or if laying down some command to servants or children, he says, "These are my words." But should he speak of everything he says, his share in a conversation, the stories he tells, the poems or essays he may write, as "my words;" we should not only wonder at the stilted style he had adopted, we should gradually come to pay slight regard to what he intended to be his most solemn attestations.

The term "word" is itself a dubious one, varying in meaning from "vocable" to "utterance." The Bible usage aims to preserve for it the latter signification, and even exalts the meaning from "an utterance" to "the utterance" of God. The modern Christian usage is ever tending downwards to the former insignificant meaning. It is for the sake of faith, that if we venture to speak of "the Word of God," we may use the phrase confidently and without reserve, that I venture to plead for a return to the habit of Scripture.

Article V.

By the Rev. PAGE HOPPS.

IN discussing such questions as that now under consideration, one continually finds that the first thing to be done is to press for a definition, or to question the question. In the present case, for instance, the inquiry is inevitable :—Of whom have we to think, when we ask, " In what sense, and within what limits, is the Bible regarded as the Word of God?" Regarded by whom? Are we discussing what the majority think,—what in the main is held—what, in short, is orthodox or authoritative? I should prefer to put the question thus :—*In what sense, and within what limits, is the Bible the Word of God?* and from that point of view I shall proceed to consider it.

Everybody will agree with Mr. Mackennal,— Mr Holyoake would probably agree with him— when he endorses the claim on behalf of the Bible, that it occupies "a unique place in literature." It is when he accepts the statement that the Bible is " the authorised record of the way in which God communicated His will to man, and (that) it is the appointed instrument for making known that will," that many will hesitate to go with him. One can understand a man saying that, who believes still what used to be generally believed, that the Bible, from beginning to end, is a supernatural production. But Mr. Mackennal is walking on a slippery plank when he accepts the statement that the Bible is "the appointed instrument" chosen by God for making known His will, and yet limits the expression of that will to certain parts of the Book. He would confine the phrase, "Word of God," to "special revelations" in particular books, and not to everything found in those books. Jeremiah, for instance, may have here and there given a revelation from God, may here and there have contributed something to "the Word of God;" but it is, to Mr. Mackennal, "inconceivable" that Jeremiah "could have tolerated the application of it (the phrase '*the Word of God*') to the whole history in which his prophecies are enshrined, or even to his prophecies themselves as edited in a book."

If, then, we proceed to the grave question— How, then, can we tell when a prophet or the writer of any Old Testament book is giving us a revelation or uttering "the Word of God"? the answer we get is an ominous one. We are referred by Mr. Mackennal to "a peculiar consciousness" in the speaker or writer, or to the assurance of the speaker or writer. Is that all? Apparently it is. But thousands of eager, devout souls have had, in all ages, "a peculiar consciousness" that God was moving them to speak; and, in every variety of warning, entreaty, and plea, have claimed to speak for God. Besides, as Mr. Mackennal himself reminds us, the prophets claimed "the Word of the Lord" for all kinds of trivialities, and, I must add, for not a few absurdities.

It seems to me, then, that if we follow Mr. Mackennal's lead, and once sever ourselves from the old uncompromising claim that the Bible is altogether a supernatural book, and all alike the "Word of God," there is no halting-place short of submitting the Bible to the verifying faculties of reason, conscience, humanity, and our own reverent trust in God. But if we do that, *this* seems to follow;—that the Bible is the Word of God only as all created things are words of His, and that it is our wisdom to mark how imperfectly His words are heard, and our duty to prove all things and hold fast that which is good.

And yet, after all, why should I speak of Mr. Mackennal's lead? As he says, "Both Dr. Leathes and Dr. Cairns are compelled, having regard to the

F

present state of science, critical and otherwise, to lay down qualifications and make reserves which, to a Jew, would have seemed not very reverent treatment of the Word of God." But we need not go so far back as that. All our theologians and critics who have any regard for "the present state of science, critical and otherwise," have "to lay down qualifications and make reserves" that would have shocked their predecessors a quarter of a century ago, or less.

I cannot help thinking, then, that real service may be done by any one who will push home conclusions, and compel people to look this matter squarely in the face. What is Inspiration? The hitherto accepted view is, that it is the supernatural or miraculous influencing of certain chosen persons, to enable them to transmit an infallible message from God; and this has always been held in company with the assertion that these persons were limited to the men who wrote the books of the Bible. God, we were told, made known His will once, and once for all; and now all we have to do is to consult "the holy oracle."

Is this view of Inspiration tenable? It is already perceived that Inspiration does not involve infallibility, and it seems to be also admitted that when we open the Bible we must distinguish and choose.

Of course we must. When objections are made to historical and scientific errors in the Bible, what more frequent than the reply, that God did not inspire men to teach Ethnology, Geology, and the like. But what of the varying standards of morality in the Bible? What of the dark and cruel things attributed to God, or done at His instigation? It is evident that we must distinguish and choose. The next step is not difficult. I regard it as inevitable. We shall have to think of God's Inspiration as we think of God's sunshine. It never goes out; it penetrates everywhere; but its brightness and blessing are ever determined by the medium, the recipient. This delicious summer air, which, incense-laden, is all about me as I write, is all-creative. It calls into being mighty forests and far-reaching harvests, but it disdains not to open the tiny eyes of the daisies in the meadow. Even so the spiritual breath of the Eternal fills the air around us, and, according to our power, each one receives it and appropriates it. Everywhere it inspires, but it does not everywhere inspire perfectly or in the same way. "The light shineth in the darkness," and the varying degrees of darkness result in varying degrees of "comprehension." Neither is this Inspiration of God for one object. It comes not only to theologian and priest; surely

it comes also to statesman and poet and scientist,
—to all who contend with darkness, and long to
come out of that darkness into the marvellous
light. That men do not come all at once to the
truth, only proves that God works in harmony
with the laws of human development; that "we
have this treasure in earthen vessels," and that God
has many things to say to us, though we cannot
bear them now.

In what sense, then, is the Bible the Word of
God? In the same sense that a rose is, or a thistle;
a sunbeam that makes a little child dance for joy,
or a lightning flash that strikes it dead. Is anything outside of God? Do we not all "live and
move and have our being" in Him? "He is not
far from every one of us." Is not that the same
thing as to say that He waits to inspire, to speak
to every one of us? Does not the "word of the
Lord" come to us now? Are all the Psalms
"inspired," and is there no "word of God" in *In
Memoriam?* Did Jeremiah transmit a "revelation"
to the men of his time, and was there never a time
when John Bright might have said "Thus saith
the Lord"? Did Moses legislate for the children
of Israel as the messenger of Jehovah, and was
Alfred the Great not sent to God's Englishmen?
Did Isaiah and Hosea and Micah speak as they were

"moved by the Holy Ghost," and did Luther and Wycliffe and Tyndale speak only from themselves? Is God near to us now, and not afar off? and if He is near to us, has He nothing more to say? or is it indeed true that "He has more light and truth to break forth from His word"? There is no possible halting-place. We must either abide by the old theory that the Bible is an entirely "supernatural" book, exceptionally inspired by God, expressly for the purpose of revealing to man His will, and of communicating to man once for all a knowledge of the truth concerning the great subjects of which it treats, or we must go on to faith in a Living God who is still educating His children, still leading them out of darkness into His marvellous light.

What is the test of Inspiration? Not eloquence, not beauty, not purity, not edification, not accuracy, if we are to abide by the theory that Inspiration is co-extensive with the Bible. These, indeed, as we all gladly testify, are in the Bible, and abound: but much else is there,—much, that is to say, which is neither eloquent, nor beautiful, nor pure, nor edifying, nor accurate. But if the tests of Inspiration *are* eloquence, beauty, purity, edification and accuracy, then we must pass beyond the limits of this noblest and best of books, to find the traces of the inspiration of the Holy One elsewhere.

If, in answer to this, it be said that that only is the "Word of God" which is absolute truth or final truth in religion, then we can only ask: Where is such truth to be found? It is admitted that such truth is not to be found outside of the Bible; but, if we turn to the Bible to find it, we find that much of what our fathers or forefathers regarded as "absolute truth" and "final truth" is now doubtful or demonstrably untrue. Qualifications and reservations multiply. Think of all the revelations of God to Abraham, Isaac and Jacob, to Joshua and Samuel, to Gideon and Ezekiel! Where men once trod unhesitatingly, and even with vehement faith, how guardedly we go! Modern civilisation, to say nothing of modern science or modern criticism, seems to be creating an absolutely new standard of things believable and unbelievable; and the influence of this upon the regarding of the Bible as in any exceptional sense "the Word of God" must be immense; it may be revolutionary.

I cannot escape from the conclusion, then, that what we have been calling "Revelation" is really discovery. Confronted with the moral, as well as with the scientific and historical, imperfections of the Bible, the defenders of the view that the Bible is a miraculous revelation from God have of late apologised for these by saying that God adapted His revelations to the people to whom they were given. It would surely be more reasonable and more reverential to say that the writers of the books of the Bible came to their knowledge and experiences just as men come to knowledge and experience everywhere—by personal thought, by voyages of discovery, by experiment. If we consider how God is dealing with us, we see that He works everywhere through man in harmony with the natural laws of his being. He gave to man by revelation no perfect final system of medicine, of government, of social economy, of mechanics, of agriculture. How much trouble, how much misery, would have been saved, we might say, if He had done so! Neither did He reveal art, and music, and poetry in perfect final forms. For all these, men have had to think, to work, to experiment. And yet, has God been excluded from these? Nay, rather, has not the Inspiration of the Eternal everywhere, and through all time, given men understanding? If all this is true and comprehensible concerning every other subject, why should it not be true and comprehensible concerning theology, or concerning what we call "religious truth"? Did God more effectively or really inspire man in the one case than the others? Why should we think so? Do we not find in the Bible precisely what we find elsewhere—manifest signs of progress, and all the indications which show that men, in regard to religious truth, as in regard to scientific and political truth, have had to find their way out of darkness into the marvellous light?

This appears to be God's way of teaching or evolving us. He has so made man, with such faculties to guide him, and with such laws to govern him, that he is perpetually going on to see more of God, of himself, and of the order and beauty and divineness of all things. The ceaseless Creator works from behind the veil, through the natural laws of man's being, slowly cleansing the vision, developing the will, perfecting the conscience, and deepening the affections. In this way all is of God, but not by miracle. Here is a pre-arranged and beautiful law at work, so that this progress on the part of man is seen to enter into that stupendous plan which is leading on to that

"One far-off Divine event
To which the whole creation moves."

How near this brings God to us!—indeed the Living God of living men, who is "not far from every one of us." Understanding this, the discoveries of man may be regarded as the revelations of God; but revelations not implying infallibility, and not involving miracle,—revelations most of all of that profound law which binds man to his actions, and which conditions all his attainments by his ever-changing plane of development. Ours, then, is not a silent Father, a banished God, audible in Jewry once, but silent in England now; speaking once to a "chosen people," but speaking now no more to His children, though they never needed Him more than now.

But, indeed, the Bible itself bears witness to this very thing,—to the ever-living and the ever-inspiring God. To what did Moses refer when, speaking for God, he said that Bezaleel had been called by name, and had been filled by God with the spirit of wisdom "to devise cunning works, to work in gold, and in silver, and in brass, and in cutting of stones, and in carving of timber;" and, indeed, that "in the hearts of all that are wise-hearted" God had put wisdom? What did he mean when he said that he would to God all the Lord's people were prophets? What is the meaning of the great doctrine of the eternal, universal, ever working Logos, "which lighteth every man that cometh into the world"? The Bible is really a witness, not to something exceptional, but to something permanent;

not to something ended, but to "a well of water springing up to everlasting life:" for all patriarchs and psalmists and prophets seem to say, not, "Lo we are unlike you, we are inspired. God is speaking to us, but not to you;" but "Lo, God is here, why do you not come and hear His voice? He is with us now and always. Listen to Him, believe, obey and live!"

In asserting, moreover, in what sense and within what limits the Bible is the "Word of God," we cannot leave out of the account one important fact;—that the Bible, given, it is said, to tell us what we could not have found out, and to settle for all time what is the truth of God, has created a variety of sects whose leading characteristic is that they differ from one another as to the meaning of this very book. The "Revelation" has revealed one thing to one man, another thing to another. The "Word of God" has said one thing to one man, another thing to another. Is that conceivable? The Roman Catholic Church, logical, consistent, and thorough as it always is, says that God has committed his supernatural and miraculous revelation to a supernatural and miraculous custodian and interpreter. That avoids or silences all questionings and dissonances. But the Protestant, with his "right of private judgment," stands more and more aghast, or is more and more puzzled, at the controversies of Christendom over the very book that was to have settled everything; and nothing is more plain to-day than this,—that the chances of Christian unity would be immensely increased if we could all be left to the voice of God speaking now in the minds, the consciences, and the affections of His children.

The singular thing is that with all this belief in the Bible as "the authorised record of *the* way in which God communicated His will to man," and as "*the* appointed instrument for making known that will," prayers are continually offered for the guidance of God's Holy Spirit. In every Established Church in England, every Sunday, prayer is offered for "the healthful spirit" of God's grace; and the prayer for "the fellowship of the Holy Spirit" is a part of the almost universal doxology of Christendom. The hymnology of all the Churches bears witness to this inconsistency between the creed of the Christian world and the trusts and longings of Christian hearts. What is the explanation? Alas, for poor human nature! The answer reveals its inherent weakness. In all ages it must have something outward to cling to,—an idol, a fetish, an altar, a pope, a priest, a confessional, a string of beads, a crucifix, a confession or catechism, a revelation. It is natural, but it belongs to our frailty, not to our force; to our childhood, not to our maturity; yes, to our unbelief, not to our faith. True implicit faith would lead to belief in the Living God, to the unseen but not unfelt Spirit. True implicit faith would teach us to walk by faith, not by sight; to trust ourselves all in all to the Father who is speaking now—to that patient and generous Being who waits to say "many things" to us when we are able to "bear them." Emerson was right. It was—

> "Out from the heart of Nature rolled
> The burdens of the Bible old."

Whatever has been may be,—and more. The old "Word of the Lord"

> "Still floats upon the morning wind,
> Still whispers to the willing mind."

Yes; still does God walk with men, the ceaseless Creator, the faithful Guide, the glorious inspirer: and we have not lost

> "One accent of the Holy Ghost."

ARTICLE VI.

BY THE REV. W. CROSBY BARLOW, M.A.

ALL that knowledge which we can so readily and certainly trace to sensation, is knowledge due to revelation. Ideas of light and shade, colour, and all visual beauty and deformity we have because a form of radient energy is self-revealing. Wave-movement speaks to the ears, and molecular motions give themselves to the finger-tips as warmth. Over and above all that is native to our conscious being, there are ideas of the most momentous import, ideas of duty and responsibility, of the Divine and of worship; these are all from the self-revealing of mind other than our own. Sense and self, and man and God, are the great sources of our knowledge, and that is not first that is spiritual, but that which is natural, and afterwards that which is spiritual.

All ideas of the supreme must be given by some form of Divine impression, by the self-revealing of God. We cannot create an idea of God and the Divine; it must be imprinted on the inner faculty, whose function is to perceive, not the visible and temporal, but that which is not seen and eternal.

At the same time it would seem to be necessary, in our present condition at least, that knowledge shall follow teaching; that dogma shall precede doctrine. Teaching gives dogma, an earthen vessel in which alone one may carry living water from the fountain. The dogma is the vessel which contains, and shapes, and often defiles the truth.

Given humanity as it is, does it not seem that children growing up untaught would remain, even in manhood, without knowledge of God, or worship, or even duty? Let the word, however, be spoken and understood, and straightway—if moral causes do not intervene—the truth uttered will be received, the dogma will contain doctrine. Thus our present mental history contains these elements; we need instruction as from without, we need moral fitness and willingness to know, and then we have within an inflowing of Divine truth. This last element is universal and perfect; the first element is practically universal, but is imperfect in most varying degree; the moral element is, as its name implies, a function of the mental and bodily habits, *mores*, of the individual.

Revelation is a fact *now*, for God, like light, is a self-revealer; and revelation is a fact of *history*, of document or tradition, as the means of that instruction, *ab extra*, without which information or internal knowledge would be impossible.

Dogma is either written, or oral, or both; that is to say, there is an external revelation, either oral or traditional. Claimants to this character are many,—the Hindoo, the Chinese, the Mohammedan Scriptures, the myths and mysteries of Greece and Rome; all these have importance and value, and they have claims to be compared, in quality and quantity of their revealings, with those documents which form the Bible, and which are specially under examination at this moment.

The Bible, we say, contains a written revelation. We go immeasurably further, and say *it contains "the Word of God."* This does not imply that the Bible is or contains the earliest verbal manifestation of God. The oldest sentence of the Bible, —" In the beginning God created the heavens and the earth,"—contains an affirmation of a supersensible universe, the heavens; of a super-physical causation, created; of a superhuman agent, God. This earliest sentence of the Bible is evidence of an anterior revelation. Let the Bible be only four thousand years old, the human race was not without a revelation before the time of Moses. The Pentateuch, indeed, is clear evidence of this in many ways. Balaam was, independently of Israel, a confessor and worshipper of Jehovah; Melchizedek was priest of the Highest; and Abram in El Shaddai worshipped the I Am.

There was, moreover, a previous *written* revelation. We have citations in 2 Sam. i., and by Joshua, of the "Book of Jasher;" the latter reference has been so misunderstood as to suggest to the heavy-leaden apologist of the Bible a miracle subversive of the universe. In the Book of Numbers we find quotations from a then existent (prophetic) "Book of the Wars of Jehovah," and also from a collection of oracular announcements of the same type apparently as those of Balaam. These books we believe to have formed parts of a more ancient Bible than that we possess. Of this, Swedenborg tells us that it was written in the style which he (as explained below) describes as distinctive of the Word of God, but that inasmuch as it was of extreme obscurity, it was first misunderstood and then falsified by the rapidly corrupting relics of the Church preceding the Israelitish. The obscurity is evident in these fragments:—

Vaheb in Supha, and the brooks of Arnon.
And the valley of the brooks that stretcheth thither where Ar lieth,
And leaneth upon the border of Moab.
And from thence to the well.
And from the well (*or* wilderness) to Mattanah,

And from Mattanah to Nahaliel,
And from Nahaliel to Bamoth,
And from Bamoth, the valley that is in the field of Moab,
To the top of the hill which looketh towards the wilderness.—Nᴀ. xxi. 14-16, 18-20.

And—

Sun, be silent upon Gibeon,
And thou, Moon, in the valley of Ajalon.
And the sun stood still, and the moon stayed
Until the people had avenged themselves upon their enemies.— Josh. x. 12, 13.

The falsification is curiously confirmed by the "Chaldean Genesis." The early chapters of the first book of Moses are part of the ancient word; the Chaldean recension of the same themes shows how already, when Terrah beyond the flood served other gods (Jos. xxiv. 2), the sacred record of creation and the flood had been marred in the interests of a new polytheism.

The corruption of the people led to their being permitted to lose their written revelation, even as the sin of Israel lost them the God-given tables of stone.

To return,—in the Bible we find a written revelation,—the Word of God. This assertion has to be examined.

A *written* revelation is a document, or series of documents, intended as a permanent ministration to men of such Divine truth as is needed, in order that they may thereby become wise unto salvation. There have been many private oracles (permit the phrase), the message of God by prophet or priest to this or that individual for this or that momentary or personal use. These we do not take into consideration now, for they have, as far as we know, perished from all earthly records, and we are concerned only with the permanent and universal, which alone is justly called a revelation.

This revelation is what we declare the Bible to contain. But such a revelation may have one of three forms—it may be translucent, or obscure, or mingled in its character, here clear and here obscure.

By a *translucent* or clear revelation is meant a document conveying teachings new to the world, or at least to its readers, and doing this in language intelligible to its full depth and throughout its whole extent. It will be understood by its writer; it can be understood by any contemporary or later student, who with fit intelligence and moral loyalty seeks to take its lessons to himself. It may be argumentative, it may be dogmatic, it must be intelligible, and it must be fixed and abiding in its meaning.

An *obscure* revelation is an inspired embodiment of Divine and spiritual truth in a document wholly or partly unintelligible to its writer and first readers. It will, therefore, be read and understood with increasing clearness through all subsequent ages.

TRANSLUCENT REVELATION. Perhaps no better illustration of this can be given than that afforded by the Pauline Epistles.

The Pauline Epistles claim to be and are a revelation. Their teaching was in the Apostle's mind most really on this ground. He was a dweller in Jerusalem where the air was still constantly moved by the rumour of all that Jesus began both to say and to do, and of all that He suffered. A Pharisee of burning zeal, he could not be without interest in the facts thus before him. The interest was quickened by Stephen's oration and martyrdom. All this was an apparatus of external fact. The vision which showed him Jesus living and exalted gave the facts a spiritual significance; what had seemed the history of a sedition against Judaism was now seen to be the embodiment of new discoveries of truth. His Gospel, as he delights to call it, was the spiritual and practical sense of a series of external deeds, discourses, and experiences of Jesus. Further breadth and depth was given to this Gospel according to Paul by visions and revelations of God, and raptures into the world normally unseen, into paradise, into the third heaven.

The revelation was intelligently received, and was to be intelligibly conveyed. The special and miraculous was lightly passed over, declared to be beyond utterance. Only in clear speech would Paul set forth what he knew. Except he utters words easy to be understood, he will be speaking into the air. Many forms of speech have signification, but speech communicates nothing unless its meaning be known. He will not pray in any speech which transcends his understanding. His hymns shall be intelligible to himself. He can use the obscurer forms of speech, but in the Church had rather utter five words intellibibly than ten thousand incomprehensibly.

To be intelligible he uses adaptation. Going to Rome he will know nothing among his brethren but the Anointed One who was crucified. When occasion served, he was delighted to advance (in the words of the writer to the Hebrews) from the principles, the first lessons of the teaching of Christ, and to go on to that which is more perfect, to something beyond the foundation truths of repentance, faith, baptism, resurrection and eternal judgment. To some he gave milk as to babes, to some meat as to men, and to the perfect he set forth that wisdom of God which was revealed to him by that Spirit which searches and reveals even the deep things of God. By adapting his speech to his hearers he constantly sought to make his revelation translucent or clear.

Such revelation, however, presupposes an anterior revelation. A clear speech is made in intelligible words. Words are such only when they are the vocal symbols of knowledge already possessed. Clear speech on Divine subjects, whether it be "wisdom" or "the sincere milk" of sacred teaching, presupposes ideas of spiritual and Divine facts, and thus implies an anterior revelation. This is universally true of the translucent inspired statement. No amount of regress will enable us to avoid the necessity of admitting some first revelation not given in words of other than spiritual significance.

The Epistles, then, which are before us, presuppose an amount of spiritual idea already in possession of men, of which we can form no adequate estimate. They are further marked by large citation of previous documents. These citations are peculiarly interesting. They are derived from the life of Jesus, and from Old Testament Scriptures. The biographical citations are of the same class as those facts which were abundantly present in the mind of Saul of Tarsus when ignorantly, in his unbelief, he persecuted Christianity. The superficial sense of the facts must needs be transcended before their spiritual value could be perceived. So also with the citations from Jewish Scripture. They are constantly used in a non-natural sense. See the references made to the unmuzzled ox, to manna, and water from the rock, to Abraham, Hagar and Sarah, &c. These references seem to usurp the Scriptures of the Jews in a sense in which they could not have been written or read by those to whom they were first given. Thus the clear revelation of the Pauline Epistles, which from its clearness must rest upon an anterior (more or less) obscure revelation, is made to rest on the visible facts of the life of Jesus interpreted spiritually, and especially on citations from the Old Testament adduced as from an obscure revelation, in which the genuine sense differs widely from the sense contained in the letter.

The translucent revelation, which aims at intelligibility and rests on an obscure revelation, is, moreover, necessarily imperfect. It is adapted to its readers,—only occasionally, and on only some few points, does it speak "wisdom" as to "the perfect." It is limited also by the writer's possibilities. No one man has ever possessed all the truth on any themes, natural or supernatural; and only so much as a man knows can he reveal, even to the fittest audience. He occasionally confesses that he is without Divine certitude. If he "*thinks*" that he is right on questions of temporary and temporal duty, if he thus doubts his knowledge on things that have to do with earth, how can we suppose him taught without limit on heavenly things? He has confessed his information limited. He has proved it defective also, as in his evident belief in the instant nearness of the Lord's second advent, and that in a personal manifestation. His theme is, the Almighty who cannot be sought out to perfection; his subject contains unsearchable wisdom, and includes the love that passes knowledge.

As such a revelation cannot be perfect amid such limitations, so neither can it be *final*. Only that can be given which is at the moment receivable, and the receptive capacity of the human race is as much a matter of gradual development as is that of an individual. Only that will be offered by Divine providence which *can* be received with immediate and eternal advantage. In a *clear* revelation only its actually and instantly intelligible meaning can be intended. If it is intended to convey more than is in its literal or other obvious sense, it is not the clear revelation of which we are treating. If, then, its teachings are limited by its obvious meaning, it can only lead us into some part of the truth, not into that "all truth" which is our destined heritage. A clear revelation, then, cannot be primal and original, it cannot be perfect, it cannot be final.

To this class of clear, secondary, imperfect and time-dated and time-limited revelations must, it seems, be ascribed the Pauline and other Epistles, and probably also the Acts of the Apostles, the Proverbs, Ecclesiastes, and perhaps other books contained in the Bible.

It is, however, already seen that other revelation than this is contained in the Bible, that is to say, if the estimate be correct which the Apostle evidently puts on the gospel narrative, and on certain ancient Jewish documents.

A digression will shorten the argument, and in this way, at least, will be serviceable. The primal revelation of God's creative work is evidently creation itself. But the *clear* revelation of this work will be sought for in systematic or popular treatises on applied mathematics and physical science. These will be intelligible to those who, understanding their terms, bring due attention to their study. But these encyclopædic treatises will not be perfect or final, and may, indeed, become obsolete, not through their being false, but through the development of scientific research on the one hand and of scientific receptivity on the side of us who are laymen in relation to this subject.

The works of God are not all always obviously intelligible, but they embody all Divine physical facts and laws, and all Divine ontological philosophy. They involve these and keep them involved until they are gradually evolved by successive seers and forth-speakers of Nature. May we not then state a proportion in these terms? as the Works of God are to our highest scientific treatises, so is the Word of God (if this be discoverable) to the Apostolic word or other translucent revelation.

The PRIMAL REVELATION, then, must have been *obscure* in this sense;—given before the mind of man was filled with large and copious spiritual ideas, it necessarily preceded any extensive vocabulary of such terms as have been differentiated for the expression of notions connected with the Divine. Thus its literal sense would, of course, be limited to words of material, mundane signification. Its inner sense would be intelligible only as our race and its members, individually grew in insight and in power to keep God and the things of God in their mind.

The absolutely primal revelation was probably subjective and individual. The earliest devout men were, by reason of their nearness to innocence, to purity of heart, able to see God in His works and to rise from Nature to Nature's Lord.

The *first* written revelation, as we have seen, is *not* extant, is represented by only such fragments as we have referred to above. A beautiful illustration, however, of its nature and form is given by many of the words of the Lord Jesus. Speaking humanly, He, as a man of His times, could and often would, use the theistic and spiritual vocabulary of His contemporaries; but on examination we find that all the characters of the obscure revelation are found in many at least of His discourses. In conversation with Nicodemus there is scarcely a word used whose prime sense is not mundane. The dicta on the new birth and on the coming and going of the wind, the Spirit, are *to us* clearly spiritual, but to their first hearer were earthly things which he could neither understand nor believe. He was receiving a new, but as yet an obscure, revelation.

The words of Jesus, indeed, seem on superficial examination to belong to the class which we have called "mixed." Jesus spoke of His going to the Father, and His disciples could not tell what He was saying; again He said, "I came forth from the Father, and am come into the world: again I leave the world, and go to the Father." Then His disciples said, "Now speakest Thou plainly and speakest no parable." It is, of course, to that which is not clear that our attention must at present be directed. We observe, then, that the revelation in the words of Jesus was often not understood. He would raise the destroyed temple, He said, in three days. Bystanders exclaimed that its building had occupied forty-six years. It is explained, however, by the Evangelist that He was speaking of His body as a temple. How often do we find His very disciples misapprehending His meaning; He spake, for example, of the doctrine of the Pharisees, and they thought He spake of the leaven of bread.

He even intended that His words should rather conceal than clearly exhibit the truth, according to a law long before uttered by Isaiah, "Lest men should understand with the heart and should convert :" to many it was not yet given to know the mysteries of the kingdom. Partial unfoldings Jesus, however, gave to the inner circle of His hearers, and showed them that the whole of His teaching was, in reality, by parables, and that in all that He said He was uttering things that had been kept secret from the foundation of the world.

He gave, indeed, explanation again and again to His disciples, but even then they understood but in part. They did not, indeed, apprehend the literal sense of His references to the decease to be accomplished at Jerusalem, and at best their understanding, their knowledge of Him, was only after the flesh and not after the spirit. Yet how plainly did He liken His words to the recognised form and presence of a man. What we see when we look upon a brother is flesh, it is mundane, and in itself is not living; it is the spirit which quickens the mortal frame, and this is the genuine, living manhood. So likewise the genuine, living meaning of His words is somewhat hidden beneath the earth-spoken, mundane elements of speech : "My words are spirit and they are life."

His words, because obscure, because they contained other meaning than was explicitly uttered, were capable of keeping for man an infinite instruction. He promises that His Spirit shall lead into all the truth, and that not by constant new documentary revelation, but by the unfolding of the previously unsuspected contents of His words. "He shall not speak of Himself, but whatsoever He shall hear He shall speak . . . . . He shall take of mine and shall shew unto you."

Of course we cannot understand in any narrow sense the "words of Jesus;" not the *logia* only, His sayings but also His deeds and whole history, and even every Divine Word, is His utterance, whatever the date or manner of its appearance in the written word. All this is parable; all is obscure in some degree; all is the gift, concealedly, of the Eternal wisdom; all is included in those things of Jesus, the unfolding of which shall be the means of leading His people into all the truth.

We turn, then, to documents *older* than the Gospel narrative. And first we remark that Moses did not, for aught we can see, understand the whole contents of his own writings. Did he see that the name God of Abraham, of Isaac, and of Jacob, was a pledge of resurrection and an irrefutable evidence that it takes place immediately on the completion of that process which we call death? Did he see any spiritual identity between Sodom and Babylon and Egypt? He did not know, we may safely say, did not know a tithe of that significance of the Law as given on Sinai which has been in part unfolded in the Epistle to the Hebrews. Nor can it be believed that he recognised the imperfection of his portrayal of the character of Jehovah, or that he suspected that his reading of the law, even on some vital points of morality, was, in the letter of the word, but a concession to the native perversity of the people, to their hardness of heart. He certainly did not know how largely it might be true of his writings that the letter killeth, and that it is the Spirit that giveth life.

It is true that some of these peculiarities of the Pentateuch are very startling as attaching to a Divinely-inspired revelation. There are yet others worthy of note. The very histories of the Word may or may not be literal records of fact. The history of the Exodus is questioned; in the Book of Judges we are reminded of the myths of early Rome; the stories of creation, of the fall, of the deluge and of Babel, are certainly not literally accurate, and possibly many later narratives may be correct records of traditional beliefs without being scientifically accurate presentations of historic fact.

Again, the Psalmists could not anticipate the full meaning to be discovered in their poetic statements of their hopes and fears, and whole meditative and emotional experience. Even so the prophets spoke for the days in which they spoke, and scrutinised their utterances, seeking to know what time and what manner of time was indicated in the words that came forth under a Divine impulse that they could neither resist nor interpret.

If these books, then, be a revelation at all, they certainly are obscure, and as surely they must, by lapse of time, become less so.

But *why should they have been thus obscure?* The answer to this question is obvious. All teaching proceeds from the known towards the unknown, and that by short steps, such as are possible to the pupil under instruction.

It was, then, important that every message should start from that point to which its hearers had already attained, and that its obvious sense should be such as to give them precisely the needed instruction, without going beyond that which could be practically adopted for the amendment of life. The Bible can directly give dogma only and incentive, the truth becomes internally known in the obedience we yield to the incentive, the workful attention we give to the dogma. Hence the letter of a new revelation always adopts as starting-point the point to which its recipients can attain at the time. Just as the world speaks to me in terms of the science which I know (including my very errors) and leads me into completer knowledge, so, not in the Word only, but in all Divine providence, the Lord's manner of working is rather to lead us first by and then from our errors, than to contradict them at once by broad statements of the truth. Thus it is no part of the evidence of the Divine Word that it shall be immaculately accurate in its letter, but that while its letter is often such as man's ignorance and hardness of heart demand, it shall, even in the letter, lead us on to salvation, and shall contain within the letter all the treasures of both wisdom and knowledge.

The Word of God and the Works of God are, then, two revelations having the same Author, and evincing not likeness only, but even *unity*. The Works are the alphabet, which becomes vocal and significant in the Word. The Works of God are divers manifestations of His wisdom and love conspiring to the use and service of man in the physical sphere of his life. The Word of God is a fuller setting forth of that same love and wisdom, and of their unity in the realm of our spiritual nature and its laws.

Causes and effects always correspond. Everything in the physical universe corresponds with something in the first cause. Everything in the spiritual world corresponds with something in the one infinite Spirit, of whom are the spirits of all flesh. And furthermore and necessarily, there is intimate connection and close correspondence between things material and things spiritual; so that the mention of a mundane thing is often obviously equivalent to the mention of a spiritual thing.

This principle lies at the base of most of what is popularly called figurative language, the pictorial setting forth of what is not seen. We are so familiar with this fact and law that we never understand literally such phrases as "a man of keen insight," "a broad thinker," "mental thirst," "the finger of God," "the dark places of the earth." In all these cases a meaning which is spiritual is expressed by a phrase which is mundane. This is the method adopted in the Divine Word in giving a revelation in which an instantly intelligible, literal sense is at one with a temporarily hidden, and infinite internal wisdom.

The law of correspondence is, of course, the law in which the Work of God and the Word of God find their unity. It is a universal law and is eternal.

The prophetic writers used this law most likely without a conscious recognition of it, or it may have been partially known to them. Indeed, in some degree all men, everywhere, recognise the principle in certain of its details of application. A man *sees* when he understands, the obedient is one who *hearkens* to the voice of his Lord, we *taste* and see how good is the Lord. Our beliefs are, or should be, well *founded*, we *advance* in civilisation, we *labour* after mental *culture*, and so on, indefinitely.

Time was when it was, at all events by some,

distinctly recognised that the Word was significant by correspondences being used at once to cover and to reveal spiritual realities.

The Apostolic word abounds in evidence that Paul and his brethren knew of this law, and could and did employ it to some extent in their readings of the prior Word of God. Origen far more extensively applies the principle. Hermas and Bunyan, in their visions and similitudes, invert the application of the law and strive to express the spiritual in terms of the natural.

We are not now, however, to trace the history of the knowledge of correspondence to its cessation and its restoration. Suffice it that the knowledge is restored, and is so offered to us that we may find the book unsealed; and may find in the seeming record of creation an account of the new birth; in the history of the Exodus, a rationale and prophecy of the "Pilgrim's Progress," and the internal history of the Spiritual Church; and everywhere a revelation of Jesus incarnate and glorified, for the testimony of Jesus is the spirit of prophecy.

We have, then, besides the Apostolic word and its kindred books in the Old Testament, a series of books which constitute the veritable Word of God, namely, the Pentateuch, Joshua, Judges, Samuel,

Kings, the Psalms and the Prophets, the Gospel and the Revelation.

To these add connective and confirmatory histories, as Ruth, Chronicles, Ezra, Nehemiah and Esther, with Job and the Song of Solomon, dramatic works which are in part, at least, imitative of the style of the Word.

The Word itself stands out from all these, even from the inspired Apostolic Word.

It is distinguished by its having a literal sense of form, specially adapted to the scene and time of its publication, and, furthermore, interior teachings which may be thrice read, as teachings for the individual or for the collective religious life (these form the *spiritual* sense), and for its continuous teaching about the Lord before and during and since the incarnation.

These senses differ; the literal is the temporary, and is marked by its date and scene, being always closely adapted to the time of its appearing, insomuch that its morality and its general character are in agreement with its authors and contemporary readers. The spiritual sense is eternal and has no date of time or place; it always and everywhere has been and is becoming true. It is present in every syllable, and renders the whole Word of God Divine, even letter by letter. It is an infallible teacher, though the teachings derived thence depend on the spiritual condition of the taught, as the quantity and wholesomeness of water from a pure fountain will be limited by the cleanness and size of the vessel into which it is drawn. The Word, consequently, by its literal sense, is an *ad interim* teacher; while men are but natural it talks with them of Egypt and its bondage; of Canaan and its milk and honey; and by the records of patriarchs and kings, by the myths of prehistoric times, by the emotional life of Asaph and David, by the visions of the prophets, by the life of the Incarnate and by the Apocalypse of His glory, it moves them to the spiritual life. During all our progress to this higher life it is an *attendant* teacher, for ever making clear the path of the heedful. Here, also, and hereafter, when we with angels desire to look into the things that are written, it is, and will be, a perennial fountain of wisdom like to the holy waters from the sanctuary, waters to swim in, a river that cannot be passed over.

This river is, in fact, the Word itself. It is in the perfect life, the river parted into four heads, giving wisdom and reason, understanding and learning; it is the refreshment of our pilgrimage, drinking of it by the way, we lift up the head; it is the purity and gladness of our social religious life, a river the streams whereof make glad the city of God; it is the healer of all disease, it fertilises barren natures, it quickens the dead, it is itself full of life, and only the utterly, obstinately evil are beyond its healing power. The marshes are given to salt.

It is the presence amongst men of the Spirit of Jehovah, impulsive to noble deeds as that Spirit was in the cases of Othniel, Jephthah, and Samson; educative to spiritual accomplishment in the Divine service, as Bezaleel was by the Spirit of God filled with wisdom, understanding, knowledge, and all manner of skill for working in gold, silver, brass, jewels and timber, even in every good work whereby the house of God is builded amongst men; and it is unlimited in teaching to all those who yield themselves for the mission of God, for he that is sent of God speaketh the words of God, for God giveth not His Spirit by measure.

This, then, is briefly an answer to the question of the meaning and extent of the phrase, Word of God, as spoken in connection with the Bible; and this answer is one which does not impair the general estimate in which the Bible is held. For the New Church the Book of Ruth is as instructive as for the Old; the Proverbs are as full of practical wisdom, the Acts as valuable from their lessons of Providence, and the Epistles for their unfoldings of the first outcome of the gospel life of Jesus. Whatever lessons have been learned from Moses and other histories, from Psalms, Prophets, Gospels and Revelation, these lessons are intact and are prized; while, if our doctrine be correct, within the clouds of the letter we may see a bright light, even the Son of Man, coming with clouds and great glory. And we may hope finally to find true as a truth of experience, that the Word which in the letter has been made flesh is indeed living and with us, that same Word which in the beginning was with God, which is God, by which all things are made.

Article VII.

By the Rev. Prof. G. W. OLVER, M.A.

THE design of this Symposium is, as I assume, to bring before its readers a clear statement of some of the many answers which may be given to the question proposed. For this reason, I do not share the difficulty which Mr. Hopps has found in its form. No one of the previous writers had professed to decide the sense in which the Bible *is* the Word of God; but only to say in what sense it is so regarded by himself, and perchance by others whom he may unwittingly represent. Mr. Hopps must not be supposed to claim any higher authority for his own conclusions. Certain it is that this paper can only be taken to express the sense in which, and the limits within which I, myself, regard the Bible as the Word of God.

Mr. Mackennal demurs to the use of this title in its application to the Bible as a whole, and especially to the New Testament. He would have it restricted to special revelations. That the expression was used by the prophets when they wished to emphasise the fact that they spoke and wrote under Divine authority, need not be denied. But it is not, therefore, necessary to admit that in its modern use, it is borrowed directly from the Old Testament writers. If they could say, "The Word of Jehovah came unto me;" St. Luke could also say, "The Word of God came unto John the son of Zacharias in the wilderness." Jesus Himself could say, "The Word which ye hear is not Mine, but the Father's which sent Me." In His last recorded prayer with His disciples He said of them, "I have given them Thy Word." So, also, the Apostles prayed, "And now, Lord, grant unto Thy servants that with all boldness they may speak Thy Word" (Acts iv. 29). They proclaimed "the Word which God sent" (Acts ix. 36). "The Word of the Lord was published throughout all the region" (Acts xiii. 49). Thus, too, it is "the Word of God" in Acts vi. 2; Eph vi. 17; 1 Peter i. 23, 25. With St. John it is likewise "the Word of God," and also, "the message which we have heard of Him and declare unto you" (1 John ii. 14; i. 5).

It cannot be necessary to refer any further to the usage of New Testament Scripture in order to justify the custom of calling the Bible "the Word of God," so far, at least, as they are concerned who accept the Bible as the divinely authorised record of a message from God, for and to mankind. Continuing, therefore, so to think and speak of it, I will try to tell why a special and Divine authority may be claimed for its teaching; to what this special authority pertains, and how far it extends; and what is the bearing of this authority upon the practical life around us.

If, whilst treating of these matters, I seem to roam somewhat more widely than my predecessors, let it be put down to the account of that variety which naturally belongs to a genuine Symposium.

The question concerning the authority of Holy Scripture is inseparable from that of the truth of Christianity, inseparable, therefore, from that of the Divinity of our Lord Jesus Christ. As He is the central figure and fact of Christianity, and its substantial embodiment; so this question centres in Him. Apart from Him there is no Christianity, and apart from Him there is no specially Divine authority for Scripture. At the same time I would not be misunderstood. With the New Testament before us, there are, at least, three distinct questions which may be separately raised and in their proper order separately answered. Was there ever such a message brought from God to men as that which this Book professes to record?

If so, have we reason for believing that this record is trustworthy and accurate? If it is, then beyond this accuracy, is there any special and Divine authority which belongs to the record? It will be seen at once that, as a matter of honest reasoning, an affirmative answer to the third question involves an affirmative for the two others; but an affirmative answer to the first, or even to the first and second, would not, without further inquiry, carry an affirmative for the third. It is with the third that we are at present concerned. In reality, however, an answer cannot be given without reference to both the second and the first.

Taking the New Testament Scriptures as they lie before us, we find that whilst written by different persons, they also treat of very different matters. Avowedly there is a strange commingling of the ordinary and the extraordinary, of the natural and the supernatural. In all this they give what is for the most part a personal testimony. The writers are of one mind with St. John when he says, "That which we have seen and heard declare we unto you." We find, however, that whether in writing history or in giving instruction to the churches under their care, they make frequent references to the life around them, to political events, to social and religious customs, to the habits of the people and the peculiarities of the scenes amid which they professed to move. Hence the trustworthiness of these writers as historians can be tested at many points. To such tests their statements have been repeatedly subjected, and with the result that they have been found both careful in their observation and accurate in their record. And seeing that they are shown to be such witnesses wherever they can be so tested, it is reasonable to believe that they are so at other times and with regard to other matters. Their testimony is therefore received concerning themselves, and not less concerning the natural life of Jesus of Nazareth. They saw Him and they heard Him, and they saw changes which followed the words He uttered or the actions He performed. He Himself explained the phenomena: "My Father worketh hitherto and I work." They record the words and also the fact that His foes not only took up stones to stone Him, but actually crucified Him because He claimed to be "the Son of God," making Himself "equal with God." This explanation of His natural life by the assertion of His divinity, was peculiarly His own. Jewish disciples had nothing within the range of their traditions or of their expectations which could have prompted it. It has come down to us through the ages; and science, whether critical or otherwise, has proved itself utterly unable to suggest for that human life, or for the record thereof, any other explanation which is not, morally and psychologically, infinitely less credible than the doctrine of the Incarnation. From that day to this, every great moral reformation and every widespread social benefit has had its origin in a simple dependence upon this Divine Incarnate Reconciler, and in a fearless assertion of that freedom wherewith He makes His followers free. Acknowledge His divinity, and the New Testament narrative is at least consistent; whilst the history of the last eighteen centuries is explicable both as to the blessings which have waited on the successes of Christianity, and the miseries which have arisen out of its perversion. Deny His divinity, and the New Testament is an enigma only less confounding than the facts of human life. And so we reverently bow before Him as "the Light of the world," the "Teacher sent from God," Himself "the Truth," "the Word made flesh." It is from Him as the manifested Jehovah that we trace the authority of the Bible.

So far as the Old Testament is concerned, a few words will suffice. "God sent forth His Son, made of a woman, made under the law." He was born as a Jew among Jews. Before He came and whilst He dwelt upon the earth, the Jewish people had their sacred writings—not Scriptures only, but "*the* Scriptures." These the Master used, claiming for them and their utterances the authorship and the authority of the Holy Spirit. To these He referred all whom He taught, and gave as a twofold reason for so doing, "In them ye think ye have eternal life, and they are they which testify of me." To the Hebrew Bible as it then existed and was accepted, He gave the sanction of His Divine authorisation as the one and only accredited handbook for those who sought to know the truth. How far this sanction and its consequent authority is inherited by our own Old Testament may be hereafter considered. The New Testament must next have our attention.

From its pages we learn that the Lord Jesus came in order to set up a kingdom. It was to be founded, maintained, extended and perfected by means of "the truth,"—"the things concerning Himself." The benefits of this kingdom were to be enjoyed by all who were brought into living union with Him, and to this end they were to be taught "to observe all things whatsoever I have commanded you." Moreover, as His apostles were specially chosen and appointed to be His witnesses, so were they specially endued with authority and power for the full and effectual accomplishment of their work. I need only refer to the well-known and oft-discussed passages concerning the remitting and the retaining of sins (Matt. xvi. 14; xviii. 18; John xx. 22, 23). It will be noted that the first passage is associated with a question of doctrine, and the second with one of discipline. The third was uttered when there was emphatically made over to them the gift of the Holy Spirit. It must suffice to say that these passages combine to bestow upon the Apostles a full constituent authority in all matters of faith and practice, and to assure them of that Divine indwelling and direction whereby they should be effectually guided in the exercise of this constituent authority, for the instruction and welfare of the Church of God in all the after ages. So the Apostles themselves understood their office and responsibility. In this spirit they spoke and wrote, and this Divine authority they did not hesitate to claim. And whilst they spoke, the Lord confirmed the word with signs following. And so it came to pass that the utterances of these divinely-chosen, divinely-guided, and divinely-accredited plenipotentiaries of the Lord Jesus were in their own day, and came to be in all after ages, accepted as the message from

Christ, "the Word of the Lord," "the Word of God." This is the authority which belongs to the Bible. It is the one and the only Book which is thus accredited to us by the Lord Himself as having been written for us by His own representatives, under the supervision and the direction of "the Spirit of Christ which was in them."

But here a question arises which must have attention. The authority spoken of above is claimed for the Bible as it must be defined in theological science. The question discussed in this Symposium has reference, possibly, to the Bible as generally received and used among us. The Bible, in theological science, consists of the original documents, uncopied and untranslated. The Bible of our daily life is the result of many translations of documents repeatedly copied, and, it must be added, somewhat variously copied. It must therefore be clearly understood that Divine authority cannot be claimed for anything which is not a correct translation of an exact copy of an originally authorised utterance and writing. Here is a wide field for antiquarian research and for scholarly criticism. Whenever these can establish the claim of a various reading, or of a revised translation, then the translation or the reading must be regarded as having its lawful place in "the Word of God." It must, however, be carefully noted that the *onus* of proof lies with the critics. The book has its history and its place in history. All the way down, and through the later ages especially, it has been jealously guarded and eagerly scrutinised both by friends and foes. Whoever would displace a book or a word, must bring evidence to show that the book or the word is not entitled to its place. Merely subjective criticism of the Bible will not suffice. The would-be subjective critic must needs produce some objective credential equal to that of the first preachers and writers of the truth.

It will be at once seen that I have propounded no theory of Inspiration. I have none to propound. "Men spake from God, being moved by the Holy Spirit." I accept the fact, and do not profess to explain the manner. The fact furnishes all the authority that the state of the case renders necessary. The result is a message from God. It is more. It is the one and only message so accredited to the human race as "*the* Word of God."

Does it follow that those who believe this must also believe that God never spake to or by any man or men other than those whose names are found in the Bible? Certainly not. Christians may well rejoice to believe that all through the ages the Spirit of God has prompted men to deeds and utterances which have been for man's welfare, and which will one day be recognised as His to His own glory. In these latter days, also, it is our confident belief that many are going to and fro, moved more or less by the Holy Spirit. It is not necessary to ask whether Tennyson or John Bright, whether Luther or Wycliffe, whether Wesley or Fletcher, ever spoke the truth of God, or proclaimed His word? Mr. Hopps passes by the real question. Is, or was, any one of these men of power openly accredited as the Apostles were by the Lord Himself as having authority to declare truth for the guidance of His Church? The Evangelists and the Apostles spoke and wrote truths which had never been before taught. These truths were found to be in accordance with previous revelation, but they had been none the less hidden. Yet the Apostles did not hesitate to claim Divine authority for their teaching, and their claim was admitted by those who saw and heard them. As for our modern teachers, it is not so. They may discourse of natural things, and we listen. Whether the truth seems to be old or new, we can test their statements and ascertain their correctness, or otherwise. But if they pass beyond the ken of natural sense and science, and so begin to deal with things which are Divine, we ask at once for their authority. If they can refer us to the only acknowledged standard, it is well. If they cannot, and if they are setting forth new doctrine concerning things beyond the limits of human observation, it is evident that they can never reasonably claim for their utterances the homage due to a message from God. This the Apostles could do, and did, and their risen Lord confirmed their word. As to all other teachers, there may be truth in their utterances, but their utterances are not the word of God.

Mr. Hopps finds a difficulty in the fact that interpretations of the Bible differ with different persons and at different times. But then he himself points to another fact which explains all this, although he seems to do so unconsciously. He says rightly, that God did not give to man by revelation a perfect final system of medicine, of mechanics, or of agriculture; and he asks why it should not be as true and as credible that God has acted in the same manner as to theology. The answer is, that the Divine method is, in this matter, the same with reference to both medicine and theology. He has not given by revelation to man a "perfect final system" in either. He has given, in both, the materials out of which, if ever, a perfect final system must be built up. But there is a difference. Medicine has to do with things which are within the range of human observation, and with truths which are within the range of human discovery. Its facts are before us in the works of God, in what we call Nature. Theology has to do with many things which are beyond the range of human observation, and with truths which man could never have discovered. And as in daily life we are constrained to rely upon testimony as to all matters which are outside of our own personal observation; so here, as to all matters outside of human ken, we are dependent upon Divine testimony, and that is revelation. For this reason it is that "a rose or a thistle" is not, as Mr. Hopps supposes, the Word of God in the same sense as the Bible is.

Nevertheless the Bible is to theology what Nature is to medicine. The statements of the former in their relation to theological science correspond to the facts of the latter in their relation to medical science. They must be observed, interpreted, compared, and systematised. In both Nature and the Bible there is truth absolute and abiding. But men differ in their observations, their interpretations, and their systems. Moreover, the same men differ at different times. So it must ever be. Medical science is ever varying, but the truth in Nature is unchanging. Theology is ever varying, but the truth in Scripture abideth for ever. Scientific change in medicine does not take away from the sufficiency of Nature; nor does scientific change in theology take away from the sufficiency of revelation. And if it be true that the scientific expression of any law in medicine must be for ever open to revision, and every system of medical science be open to change and reconstruction as the study of Nature is pursued; it is no less true of theology that the continued study of the Word of God must leave every scientific dogma open to a corresponding revision and amendment, and every system of theology open to change and, if need be, to reconstruction. Nevertheless, in the one case the Works of God, and in the other the Word of God, is the ultimate and supreme standard of appeal. Both equally express the truth of God; but each has its own message.

For practical ends there is a difference which is of infinite importance. For natural purposes it would scarcely avail if the sufferer from disease were told to go and study Nature in order to find a remedy for his ills. He must have a man like himself who, by his superior and scientific acquaintance with the human body and with medicine, may explain the disease and provide the remedy. Medical science must intervene between the sufferer and the cure. In dealing with spiritual maladies it is not seldom otherwise. I do not say that here also scientific knowledge of human nature and of theology, brought to bear by a human teacher, may not often be useful. Nor will I say that practical experience, apart from definitely scientific knowledge, may not be of great service in either the physical or the spiritual need. But when a sinner desires salvation, when the honest doubter seeks rest, he may go to the Bible and his God. As he reads,—earnestly and prayerfully pondering that which he reads,—the original Revealer will teach him the way of life. He may never attain to theological science, and his beliefs, so far from being harmonised and systematised, may be strangely disconnected and even logically incongruous. Nevertheless, his spiritual disease is cured, and his spiritual life is nurtured and perfected; for in the study of the Word he has found communion with God. The Spirit of truth guides him into the whole truth, so far as his own life-wants are concerned. He cannot define for you his creed, but he has found the Christ. In this also we rejoice. That which Mr. Hopps regards as an inconsistency, is rather the logical outcome of the theory which affirms that the Bible is the Word of God. "The natural man knoweth not the things of the Spirit of God, for they are foolishness unto him," even though he reads them in the Bible; "neither can he know them, because they are spiritually discerned." And so every learner must come to the one unseen Teacher and rely upon Him. With the open Bible as his one handbook, every "disciple indeed" will find that Mr. Hopps has uttered truth when he says, "True implicit faith would lead to belief in the Living God, to the unseen but not unfelt Spirit. True implicit faith would teach us to 'walk by faith, not by sight;' to trust ourselves all in all to the Father, who is speaking now—to that patient, generous Being who waits to say 'many things' to us when we are 'able to bear them.'"

To many it will be evident that there are details which I have not attempted to discuss. We hear much of difficulties arising out of the history and the supposed ethics of the Old Testament. I confess that if they were more and far more startling than they are, it would disturb me but little. The believer in Christ is in no way called to profess that he can solve all difficulties and harmonise all statements in the Book of Revelation, any more than the believer in a Creating Father, or the believer in an uncreated universe, can solve all difficulties and harmonise all facts in Nature. Daily life does not depend upon a perfected science, but upon the personal use of knowledge acquired, and personal obedience to laws that are ascertained. The salvation of a sinner does not depend upon a perfected theology, embracing within its compass a perfected criticism and exegesis of Scripture, but upon a personal use of the truth which has been learnt and a personal obedience to the directions which are set forth. A practical faith in a living Saviour, ever present and always sufficient, is the only path of life revealed for man. There are facts in geology, concerning which the most haughty scientist can only guess the explanation. There are facts in Biblical exegesis, also, for the explanation of which theologians must wait. The presence of the former does not disprove that the heavens and the earth are the embodiment of the Creator's will; and the presence of the latter cannot disprove that the Holy Scriptures are the authorised message of His grace to man. Men wrote them under His direction or supervision, and He gave His sanction to that which they had written. His authentication was recognised by His followers. Ecclesiastical authority could never add thereto or take therefrom. Councils have recorded history, but they never could attest inspiration. Churches may formulate dogmas, but they never can supplement revelation. These may come and go, but the Word of the Lord abideth for ever; and this is the Word which by the Gospel is preached, and by the Bible is declared unto us.

Article VIII.

By the Rev. EDWARD WHITE.

THE *Spectator* newspaper recently remarked that the establishment of some defensible doctrine on Inspiration is the first condition of a successful war against modern scepticism. Without admitting that the test of spiritual truth is the satisfaction of sceptics,—not a few of whom are the most unreasonable of mankind,—I agree with some preceding writers in thinking that the principal difficulties felt by honest readers of the Bible, both believing and unbelieving, are occasioned by the old ecclesiastical theory of Inspiration; and that such difficulties are either alleviated or removed by reversing the usual method of apologetics, and postponing the adoption of any theory of inspiration until the Scriptures have been studied apart from such traditional theories. A doctrine of inspiration is the last and not the first lesson of a faith formed inductively on the evidence.

The ecclesiastical idea of "the Bible" is that it is One Book, consisting of many parts, each of which has received the sanction of the Church in the earlier Christian ages as authentic and divinely inspired; so that the whole Hebrew and Greek Bible, from Genesis to Revelation, is alike and equally the Word of God.

I. The first step towards a solution of the question now before us is, I think, to set aside at once this, and all other authoritative Church theories on Inspiration, from the Roman down to the Puritan; and to fall back for a basis on the statements given by the Scripture writers themselves on the measure and quality of their own inspiration. Surely no one can be justly required to believe concerning "the Bible" as a whole, more than its writers individually or collectively declare respecting themselves. Let us, then, steadfastly adhere to the statements respecting each separate work in succession made by its own writer, *taking our estimate of the authority of each book from what the writer himself says of it, or some one subsequently claiming to speak with Divine authority,*—and not from what uninspired churchmen in subsequent ages have maintained on their behalf collectively.

The first result of this method will be that, passing by the opinions of ecclesiastics in the third and fourth centuries, who formed what is termed *the Canon*, and co-ordinated all the scattered Scriptures into one collection, called afterwards *the Bible*—now regarded by Christendom as produced by a homogeneous theopneustic process, we throw ourselves back into the age immediately following the events recorded, and consider the phenomena thus presented to us.

Under these conditions the modern and now dominant idea of *one Book*, called "the Bible" or "New Testament," vanishes immediately out of the field of view. The idea of the Bible as one all-inspired Book no longer exists. It is not found in any of the scattered original writings of Christianity. It is the product of a later age. A collection of the four Gospels, and of the apostolic Epistles, enforced in every word as authority over men's consciences by an indiscriminate doctrine on their inspiration, formed no part of the earliest Christianity, and therefore should not form the foundation or first principle of ours.

The formation of the Canon, as a series of books, consisting of so many and no more, was essentially a human work resting on the literary and spiritual ability of the churchmen of the third century. The conception of a homogeneous verbal inspiration as attaching to each and all of these books, was an additional ecclesiastical opinion *not resting on any inspired authority*, not asserted in any of the books declared to be canonical, and expressing only the judgment of the canonists. There was for several generations a difference of opinion on several of the books finally received as canonical, and to the present day some of the Epistles are not comprised in the versions of the second century.

If we thus relegate the notion of canonical Scripture as a unity, from the foremost to the hindmost place in our method of study, postponing the consideration of that wonderful internal and spiritual unity of testimony, which gave rise to the conception of the Biblical unity,—what have we left?

The idea of "the New Testament," as written or printed in one volume, has vanished. What then remains to us, conceived of as contemporaries with the writers? A number of distinct and separate compositions, writings as distinct as those of the authors of Greece or Rome, coming to us each with its special evidence of authenticity, and making its own claim upon our belief, without the faintest reference to any other authorities. If we could read these books, now for so many ages written or printed together in one volume, in their original condition, as so many distinct treatises, independent in their authorship, we should find ourselves in much closer relation with the original facts than when we read them as the "Bible" or the "Testament," and look at them all together in the light of a Church theory respecting the mode of their common production. If we could thus read, as distinct and separate memoirs of our Lord Jesus Christ, the four Gospels, coming to us in books as distinct and independent as those of Cicero, Virgil, Suetonius or Tacitus, apart from any idea of a Canon, we should see the absurdity of claiming for the mode of their production more than they each claim for themselves; or of asserting for all alike some uniform measure and quality of "inspiration."

This is an after-thought of the Church, which only gradually grew up in early ages, but has reached its consummation in the days when Protestants supposed that they required an absolutely infallible "Bible" with which to fight the Roman infallibility.

The truth is that Christianity has in every age been greatly sacrificed to its many artificial defences in Church and State, and especially to this defence of an authoritative Canon, with its correlative notion of a uniform verbal *theopneustia*. Christianity was very well able to take care of itself as the "weakness of God," without these ecclesiastical additions and buttresses to its authority. Nor do we lose anything by the proposed method of regarding these records. For how can the faith of unlearned persons rationally rest for its deepest foundations on any ancient human authority determining the precise number of treatises which shall form the "New Testament" or "Bible"? How can the unlearned know whether the particular councils which settled the Canon were composed of wise or partially illiterate and foolish men? How can the unlearned know whether subsequent generations have been right in their notion of the *equal verbal inspiration of all these writings* so incorporated in the Canon? If there be no other method of reaching truth by which men can learn for themselves divine realities, like the Samaritans who having seen Jesus for themselves, said, "Now we believe, not because of thy saying,"—the unlearned are in an evil case.

But it will be said, perhaps, "If you take away from the Church its primary idea of the 'New Testament' as a unity, and abandon the idea of equally inspired canonical Scripture as its uniform characteristic, you take away from the people the foundation of faith, and *nothing is left* as the basis of belief for any man except Church authority or his own reason." This pernicious delusion deserves the strongest contradiction. If the whole New

Testament were blotted out of human memory tomorrow, with the exception of a single Gospel (suppose that of St. Matthew), and that Gospel came to us floating on the stream of general history just as an ancient work, without any recommendation whatever from Church authority, and without any annexed theory as to its inspiration, but handed down through the centuries as the books of Tacitus have been handed down to us; there would exist, in the self-evidencing worth of that single writing, an amply sufficient basis for faith in Jesus as the Son of God and Saviour of the world. The only question would be, Is this wonderful and holy narrative of the teaching, the miracles, the life, the sufferings, the resurrection of Jesus of Nazareth—true? and the reply must be determined primarily, not by any notion of inspiration, or by reference to other books, or to a Canon, but first of all by its own interior qualities; and secondly, by its contemporaneous and subsequent reception as an authentic story, which is a question not for learned men only. So far is it from the truth that a theory of verbal inspiration is any aid to faith in relation to historical books, that "you must first ascertain," as the late Archbishop of Canterbury declared in his latest Charge, "their historical truth by the ordinary methods of criticism, before any question of their inspiration can even arise." If you have not ground to believe in the historical truth of the four Gospels from intellectual and moral reasons, of the same class which compel you to believe in the general veracity of Livy or Tacitus, or Lingard, or Macaulay, you cannot possibly attain solid belief in them by setting up a doctrine of verbal inspiration. You are building on the sand, or in the air. But if you already have reason to believe, from their tone and style, that Matthew and Luke are thoroughly honest and well informed, and above all God-fearing writers, recording the substantial truth, you gain nothing by the notion of a Canon, or by the gratuitous hypothesis of verbal infallibility as the law of the composition. It is assuredly a great material convenience to possess the four Gospel histories in one volume; but from the beginning it was not so, and it somewhat diminishes the weight of their coincident testimony, which would come out all the more forcibly, if they were read as four separate biographies. If the works of Suetonius and Tacitus and other Roman historians had always been bound up together in one "book" or "Canon of Roman history," it would have partially weakened in the public mind the force of their independent testimony respecting the character of the Cæsars. Physical unity is not always strength.

It is therefore sufficient to believe just as much as each of the Evangelists severally tells us respecting the mode in which his " Gospel " was produced; and the silence of each in turn respecting any sort of supernatural impulse to write it, or of any dynamical supernatural control in writing it, is in exact conformity with all the internal phenomena of the four compositions. With St. Luke's preface before us—describing the process of collecting his materials from eye-witnesses as altogether in accord with that pursued by every other historian—a description which was almost profane and injurious to God, if he were conscious of writing under a direct Divine impulse, or under infallible guidance,—nothing can be conceived more gratuitous than the allegation that he was a mere pen of the Omniscient Spirit, by whom he was preserved from every minute mistake or partial representation. While, on the other hand, nothing can be conceived of as more convincingly truthful than the general agreement of four contemporary narratives, by independent writers, respecting the teaching, miracles, death, resurrection and ascension of Jesus, our Lord. The theory of a dynamical inspiration of these four histories may

K

be at least postponed to the time when it shall appear that any one of their authors professes to write under such an influence; or until it shall appear that the four Evangelists have written in full, complete, minute and verbal agreement on every incident of their marvellous story. "The weakness of God is stronger than men."

The fundamental question for modern inquirers is, *Is the miraculous history of the Books in the Old and New Testaments substantially true?* And this question can be answered by common people quite apart from any dogma on the Canon or on Biblical inspiration. Take the historical books of the "Bible" for what they are worth as human histories. Do *they* record events truly? If they do, then the higher *dogmatic* pretentions to inspired authority on the part of Prophets and Apostles can be sustained, or rather *they follow upon the truth of* the history. If the truth of the history cannot first be made out on common grounds of internal evidence and human authentic testimony, then the whole superstructure of "Revelation" falls with it. This, I think, is the reason why the historical Gospels approach us with no claim to what is commonly called "inspiration"—(though, indeed, they breathe throughout a God-revealing spirit),— but place the facts of the Divine Revelation in

Christ before us, like ordinary historians, simply on the basis of their truth in the world of phenomena. Such a mode of reaching us first of all with the historic reality of revelation, on the human level, is in accordance with the law of continuity which prevails everywhere in the Kingdom of God. By a gradual incline, sloping upwards from the ordinary level of human history, learners ascend to a higher plane.

II. But it is far otherwise with those books of Apostolic origin which contain the *dogmatic* teaching of the Prophets and Apostles. Here we find, time after time, the most explicit and positive claim to speak *to believers* by a direct inspiration and command of God. *Thus saith the Lord*, is the perpetually recurring preface of the Prophets and Apostles in their communications. We find this alike in the pages of Isaiah, and in the Epistles of St. Paul, Peter, and John. In every one of his Epistles, St. Paul distinctly and emphatically claims to speak with the direct and infallible authority of the Risen Christ, except in two or three small matters on which he gives his "opinion." A full induction of every phrase in his writings asserting or implying such a direct inspiration of God, would require an abstract of nearly half his writings. The whole Second Epistle to the Corinthians is an elaborate and unflinching assertion of this claim. Here, then, there is no alternative, except that of either receiving his teaching as divinely authoritative, or of rejecting it; and that must be determined by each man according to his general belief or unbelief in the history of Paul's commission as an Apostle by the apparition of Christ (thrice recorded in the narrative of St. Luke), and according to his spiritual recognition of the Divine element in this Apostle's life and writings, in which he "commends himself to every man's conscience."

III. This leads to the last point in the Scripture doctrine concerning Inspiration, which is exceedingly different from that of the ecclesiastical Canonists. These content themselves with binding together in one "book" all the histories, poems, prophecies and dogmatic writings of the men who lived in contact with the Revelation of God during many ages, and with asserting, concerning the whole collection, one simple principle of a direct verbal inspiration. The sacred writers themselves approach us each with a separate work, and with different measures of claim to direct inspiration; though all alike profess to speak the truth. But one and all insist on a remarkable complex definition of Divine Revelation as a whole; that it consists of three parts, one of *facts* in the world of phenomena, which can be duly and sufficiently reported by honest historians; the second, of God-given *ideas* in the world of thought, explaining and enforcing those supernatural facts; and the third, in the verifying and interpreting faculty bestowed on the divinely touched soul. *They shall be all taught of God.* " *Every man that hath heard and learned of the Father cometh unto Me.*" " *The natural man comprehendeth not the things of the Spirit of God, neither can he know them, because they are spiritually discerned.*" The prophetic writers of the Bible insist quite as much on this universal and complementary inspiration or guidance of honest souls, as on their own. No part of the " Bible " will be effectively "regarded by its readers as the Word of God," apart from this capacity for receiving the visions of God. And when this capacity does not exist, the Church cannot apparently supplement the deficiency by any exaggerated dogma on outward Canonic Infallibility. " *The wicked shall not understand,*" and the wicked man will not understand Divine things the better for all the mechanical theories respecting " Canons " and " Bibles " written with a steady verbal "infallibility." Under such a divine personal instruction men of old were trained to be adequate historians of Christ, and to reflect His glory in the pages of the four Gospels, even when using their ordinary human faculties in co-ordinating the materials supplied by the original "eye-witnesses" and inspired ministers of the Word. Under such an instruction spiritual men now read their writings, and recognise the Divinity of the Lord whose life is there. Under such an instruction we recognise the marvellous grace of simplicity and self-oblivion which fitted the Evangelists to indite the records of the Theophany,—yes, and we perceive that inward spiritual unity of the holy writings, which does indeed interiorly organise them into a "Canon" and a "Bible" for discerning eyes—at the end rather than at the beginning of the Christian life. But apart from such a personal visitation of God, opening the inner senses and conferring spiritual insight, a man is a long way off from the knowledge of truth, notwithstanding all the well-meant but fallacious appliances of the Protestant or Roman Catholic Infallibilities. The Bible is to be reached by the masses only by translation out of "dead languages," and if a man has no means of "knowing" except by reliance on translation and professional exegesis, he remains in the school of those who "hear" rather than of those who "see." It requires inspired good sense to open the Scriptures even after they have been "translated out of the original tongues." Exegesis is ever approximative, never complete.

But how fearful the results of the coarser prevailing theories as to the "Bible;" and of its perversion as an authority, when its history as the record of a progressive and gradual revelation, first through barbaric and afterwards through civilised ages, is forgotten or unheeded. The Bible widely diffused among the homes of a nation may become a curse, or a blessing, according to our attainments in the art of handling it. Here is a mass of writing; history, poetry, aphorism, allegory, prophecy, epistle, apocalypse,—every line and word of which is supposed by many to carry with it the authority of the Infinite God, the Author of Creation. It is the work of fifty different writers, of different ages, living under different degrees of illumination, of different natural genius, education and capacity, the whole delivered in various dialects of Hebrew and of Greek, under the different styles of four dozen authors, some of them exceedingly prone to parenthesis and complication, others to a law of mental association, depending on the suggestion of the last written clause. Now it is quite conceivable that if this entire mass of "Scripture" were translated with uniform and perfect exactness into living

English,—and if, when so translated, every passage were interpreted in its original sense, according to its connection, neither adding to nor taking away from the writer's precise meaning, nor perverting it to divergent uses; if the history were treated as precedent, and the biography as example, only so far forth as the writer designed; and if the utmost attention were given to avoid all supernumerary and fallacious deductions, all inferences founded on a mistaken conversion of logic into rhetoric, or rhetoric into logic,—none but beneficial results could ensue.

But when this prolonged series of books is subject to translation into modern languages, Eastern words into the phrases and idioms of the West, sometimes at the hands of scholars devoid of " the vision and the faculty divine;"—when this large body of writing is liable at every line to the misconceptions of blundering or interested expositors; when there is no absurd perversion of its meaning by non-natural senses imposed on the plainest words for which some readers will not be ready to plead direct Divine authority;—when abolished primitive dispensations are ransacked for precedents of modern slavery, of polygamy, of cruelty in war; when the rules of conduct proper or tolerable in periods of barbarism, or of moral transition, are held up as laws of eternal obligation; when absolute statutes are reasoned out of incidental references; when great institutions are founded on single perverted texts (as on "Thou art Peter," &c.);—when enormous pyramids of inference are made to stand upside down on the apex of a single wrong quotation; when the conclusions of exact science, as in astronomy, may be set aside and condemned in favour of the "Biblical" physics of a barbarous antiquity;—when modern society may be broken into sectarian shivers by the contradictory "authority" of passages respecting a ceremonial observance imperfectly understood;—when a slavish spirit of subservience may end in the destruction alike of the reason of the teacher and the conscience of the taught; when systems of metaphysical theology, overshadowing human life with the most direful terrors, may be built up by rustics and their spiritual guides on the foundation of one wrested Epistle or one phrase in a Gospel, which is not found in the *Vetus Itala*;—in such circumstances as these it is evident that a complicated written "revelation" may become a bitter fountain, infecting with its "streams of burning pitch" every department of a life already sufficiently entangled and forlorn. There is no folly, no God-dishonouring theology, no iniquity, no sacerdotal puerility, for which chapter and verse may not be cited by an enslaved intelligence. And under these circumstances it is impossible to express in adequate terms the importance of a correct estimate and exposition of "the Bible."

Towards such a consummation the first step is, I think, resolutely to fling aside the post-Nicene theory of the inspiration of "the Bible" as a whole; to resolve this Bible into its original elements; and to regulate our view of each of these component parts by the writer's own testimony concerning the degree in which he was "moved by the Holy Ghost." And while this will modify the sense in which we shall habitually speak of the whole collection, from Genesis to Revelation, as equally, and fully, and directly, and permanently, the "WORD OF GOD," it will leave us with an ever-growing sense of the substantial truth of its histories, and I think with nothing less than an infinitely deeper and more submissive reverence than Mr. Page Hopps feels, for the *authoritative* teaching of those who were the Prophets of Judaism and the Apostles of the Gospel.

Article IX.

By Prof. ISRAEL ABRAHAMS, M.A.

IT is possible to regard this momentous subject from several distinct points of view—a fact that the present series of papers has amply illustrated. It is, therefore, as the Rev. John Page Hopps pointed out, essential to press for a careful definition of the terms of the question from the very outset. The writer whom I have just named preferred to modify the question now under discussion by the omission of the words "regarded as." From his standpoint such modification was, no doubt, necessary. Since, however, my intention is the very opposite of his; intending, as I do, to abstain, as far as may be, from intruding my own individual opinion on the readers, I prefer to take the question in its original wording:—*In what sense, and within what limits, is the Bible regarded as the Word of God?*—regarded, that is, by Jews of the ancient and modern schools. My answer to this question will be more expository than critical; and will naturally fall under two distinct heads.

1. In the Rabbinical conception, no specific distinction was drawn between the Pentateuch and the remaining portions of the Old Testament. (See particularly *Talm. Babli. Baba Bathra*, fols. 18 b, 19 a). Every part of the Bible was inspired; and the historical books, no less than the prophetical, were an integral part of the Word of God. Indeed, the authors of these two sections are sometimes considered identical, and Jeremiah, to give an instance, was quoted as the author of the Books of Kings as well as of " his book "—to use the Talmudic phrase — and of the Lamentations. David was inspired when he composed his Psalms, " aided by the ten ancients, Adam, Melchizedek, Abraham, Moses, Haimon, Jeduthun, Asaph, and the three sons of Korah," even as Moses acted under Divine influence when he wrote down the Pentateuch. Citations in the Talmud are freely made from Pentateuch, Prophets, and Hagiographa, (תורה נביאים וכתבים) as from works of equal authority. And yet questions as to the limits of the Biblical Canon were not unknown. Ezekiel and Ecclesiastes were, in the opinion of some Rabbis, to be excluded from the authorised list of Biblical books. (See *Mishnah*. Treatise Yadaim, chap. iii., § 5.) The ground for this exclusion was the supposed internal evidence of their uninspired

character. If Ecclesiastes contained glaring self-contradictions, if Ezekiel was found in total disagreement with the Pentateuch, the inspiration of whose author was unquestioned and unquestionable, neither Ecclesiastes nor Ezekiel could be, in any true sense, the Word of God. Here, then, we see established a sort of *negative* test of inspiration, a test of uncontrovertible cogency within the prescribed limits. The supposed inconsistencies of Ecclesiastes, and the seemingly erroneous statements of Ezekiel, needed, however, the exercise of very little ingenuity for their reconciliation with one another and with independent Biblical works. The former books, therefore, satisfied the *negative* as well as the *positive* tests of inspiration; and indeed there could have been no question as to their satisfying the former, had there been an entire certainty that they fulfilled the latter.

When we come to ask, as so many have asked, for the positive test of inspiration, we are met with the answer, *Tradition*. Thus, the books of the Apocrypha were not numbered among the inspired writings simply and solely because they were traditionally excluded. It may be as well to point out that the individual authorship of the various Biblical writings was not a question of much importance in this connection. This fact is not always borne in mind. When, nowadays, critics—such as Kuenen, Kalisch, and Robertson Smith—question the Mosaic authorship of the Pentateuch, the underlying inference usually is, that were the Mosaic authorship once thoroughly disproved, the theory of the Divine origin of the Law would be *eo ipso* relegated to a place among the myths of the past. The Mosaic authorship of the Pentateuch was certainly accepted by the Rabbis without question. Maimonides drew up a short list of what he regarded as the leading principles of the Jewish faith, a list that is sometimes described under the title of the "Jewish Creed." Such a title is somewhat misleading, for there is no such thing as a recognised "Jewish Creed;" but that by the way. The eighth principle enumerated by Maimonides runs thus:—"I believe with a perfect faith that the Law which we now possess is the one which was revealed unto Moses, our teacher." Still, we find an important difference of opinion with the Rabbis as to the authorship of the last chapter of Deuteronomy (or, at least, of the concluding eight verses); some authorities holding that Moses, others that Joshua composed them. Then again, the authorship of Job, and of various other books, was much disputed. But, as I have already remarked, these differences of opinion were *practically* insignificant. For if the *whole* Bible was, in all its parts, equally the inspired Word of God, it really mattered very little whether Moses or Joshua was, in this particular case, the human means of making known unto men the message of their God.

The main flaw in this method of regarding the subject, of course, seems to lie in the apparent absence of interpretation as to the meaning and reliability of the test of tradition. The answer to the difficulties which this consideration appears to suggest, will best be given when these objections are brought into relation with a similar argument in Mr. Page Hopps' paper—a paper which is in several ways remarkable. " In ascertaining, moreover, in what sense, and within what limits, the Bible is the 'Word of God,' we cannot leave out of the account one important fact;—that the Bible, given, it is said, to tell us what we could not have found out, and to settle for all time what is the truth of God, has created a variety of sects, whose leading characteristic is that they differ from one another as to the meaning of this very book. The 'Revelation' has revealed one thing to one man, another thing to another. The 'Word of God' has said one thing to one man, another thing to another. Is that conceivable ? " Mr. Hopps perceives that the Roman Catholic Church is "logical, consistent, and thorough" when it asserts that "God has committed His supernatural and miraculous revelation to a supernatural and miraculous custodian and interpreter. That avoids or silences all questionings and dissonances." In the Rabbinical theory this principle is formulated, and is carried out even more consistently. In the first place, that traditional interpretation was itself regarded as inspired, in much the same sense as the original text of the Scriptures. The "Oral Law" was as much the Word of God as was the "Written Law." "Moses received the Law at Sinai, and delivered it unto Joshua," says the Mishnah, "Joshua delivered it unto the Elders, and the Elders to the prophets, and the prophets to the men of the Great Synagogue." The "Law," herein mentioned, includes the oral traditions. The objection to this is, if the oral law was truly inspired, why was it not incorporated with the written text? If the written text was not, in itself, sufficiently explicit to be termed the whole of the Word of God, why were not those additional revelations authoritatively added, seeing that they alone could give to the written Word the character of perfection and completeness which was claimed for it? Joseph Albo, a Jewish writer of the fifteenth century, who on points such as the present takes strikingly comprehensive views, and offers peculiarly acute suggestions, gives a simple, but conclusive reply. It was, he contends, *impossible* to incorporate the oral with the written law without altogether destroying its value and thwarting its purpose. "If the inspired interpretation of the Written Law had been itself committed to writing, the same difficulty of explanation would meet us in the case of the interpretation as had rendered the latter necessary, in the first instance, for the elucidation of the written text. The first interpretation would stand itself in need of interpretation, and so on *ad infinitum.*" This, indeed, is what did happen when an attempt was made in later ages to write down the oral traditions. "The Mishnah," continues Albo, —whom I am rather freely translating,—"was the compilation of the Oral Law. So soon, however, as it was completed, doubts and difficulties arose as to its meaning. So considerable were these doubts, so perplexing these difficulties, that it was found necessary to put forward an authoritative interpretation of the Mishnah. This work was the *Gemara*, or Talmud. But the difficulties were by no means ended. The Gemara was at once found to need explanation itself. Hence arose a large number of commentators, who devoted much time and labour to the task of Talmudic interpretation. And then the commentators need explanation" (*Sepher Ikkarim*, Part III., chapter xxii.).

Having established the necessity of an oral law, such must further be an *inspired* law, to possess the requisite authority. The inspiration of the oral law was of exactly the same kind as that of the written law. Thus the Rabbis regarded as the Word of God, not only the Bible, but also the traditional explanation. Perhaps not the whole of the Mishnah was considered as inspired;[*] but Dr. Schiller Szinessy is certainly not representing the Rabbinical view when he asserts,—in his article on the Mishnah, contributed to the Ninth Edition of the *Encyclopedia Britannica*—that "There are but few cases to be found in the *Mishnah* which would critically come under the denomination of *Halakhah le-Mosheh mis-Sinai*, *i.e.*, an explanation (of a law) as directly given by God to Moses, and in uninterrupted succession received from him by the Rabbis." Nor, again, was the Mishnah the *whole* of the oral tradition. To complete the latter we must add the *Tosiphto*, which, "as its name indicates, is 'Addition,' *i.e.*, to the canonical Mishnah;"

[*] Much of it is avowedly the result of an application of the Methods of Interpretation alluded to further on. In such cases, so long as the Methods could be shown to have been properly applied, the results thus arrived at were received generally.

the *Mechilto*, a commentary on Exodus; the *Siphro*, on Leviticus; the *Siphre*, on Numbers and Deuteronomy; and the *Boraitho*, or scattered fragments. Not only was this oral explanation in itself inspired, but the earliest of those who were made its recipients, and the means of communicating it to later generations were, in so far at least as those precepts and traditions were concerned, inspired also. And hence, returning to our original difficulty, viz., in how far tradition could be a test of inspiration, we find that the objection, seemingly so fatal, has in fact no relevancy whatever. *That was the Word of God which was so pronounced by an inspired tradition.*

The matter, however, has not so far been fully analysed. There are two circumstances—important elements of the case—which must now be alluded to, and which may perhaps seem to modify considerably the Rabbinical conception of inspiration. The first of these facts is the existence of a definite code of principles for the interpretation of the Bible. These principles constitute what I may term the Logical Methods of the Talmud. There is some uncertainty as to the number and character of these principles. Thus, while Hillel enumerates seven such principles, Rabbi Ishmael on the one hand formulates thirteen, and Rabbi Eliezer ben

José, of Galilee, thirty-two on the other. These various statements can, however, be very easily reconciled (comp., *e.g.*, *Shnè Luchoth Hab-berith*, folios 389 seq.); and the enumeration of Rabbi Ishmael is adopted as the one which all authorities were agreed in recognising. Now the discussions in the Talmud, based on the text of the Mishnah, are very frequently opened by the question:—Whence did the Mishnah derive the statement under consideration? The answer to this question often amounts to the assertion that the statement of the Mishnah is a direct tradition from Sinai. But in many cases the Talmudic answer is far different. The statements of the Mishnah are shown to be derived from the written words of the Law, in accordance with the principles by means of which, in Rabbi Ishmael's language, the Law is to be explained. Thus it would seem, not that the final result was a part of the inspired tradition; but that, while the method of obtaining the result was inspired, that result itself was only arrived at by means of the discussion that had preceded. It may, however, be doubted whether this, in some cases, is really so. We frequently meet in the Talmud with the caution that no man was to apply certain, at least, of these logical methods to obtain results which were not confirmed by distinct tradition. In other words, a consistent theory of the tradition has been built up on the hypothesis that the logical methods were not what always *were* actually employed in obtaining the traditional results, but what might have been so employed, had not distinct traditions rendered such a course unnecessary.

The Old Testament, then, was, together with the Oral Traditions, in the conception of the Rabbis, the Word of God, and the whole of the Word of God. They could conceive no possibility of an addition to the Written Law, nor of the abrogation of any of its precepts. In one sense, later Jewish authorities of the greatest weight appear to have fallen away from this conception. The ninth article of the creed of Maimonides indeed asserts a belief that the Law of Moses was final and immutable as the Word of God. But Maimonides, as I have incidentally stated in a former article, did not hesitate to declare that the Levitical sacrifices, for example, were an institution of a temporary and transitory nature. There is not *real* inconsistency here. When Maimonides asserted that the Law of Moses was final, he meant the Law of Moses as he understood it; and, as he understood it, the Sacrifices were *ab initio* a temporary institution. Still, the introduction of this element—of his own individual opinion—indicates an important change in the ordinary Jewish point of view.

To return to the second of the two circumstances to which I have alluded. On reading the Bible with the assiduity and care which the Rabbis applied to the work, it was impossible for them to avoid being struck by some of the difficulties which lie upon the very surface. First, there are the anthropomorphisms of the Bible. In what sense can that be the Word of God which represents Him as seeing and hearing, as possessed of hands, as forming resolutions and then repenting of His determination? And secondly, despite the inspired oral traditions, several sections of the Bible still remained obscure and inexplicable. How was an explanation to be found for these passages? That the first of these questions attracted very deep attention may be gathered from the fact that when Onkelos or Aquilas compiled his "Targum" translation of the Pentateuch he avoided the Biblical anthropomorphisms altogether. At times he found it necessary to adopt the most remarkable circumlocutions to effect his objects, but he almost invariably succeeded in his attempt. This systematic modification is an instance and an illustration of the important Talmudic principle :דברה תורה כלשון בני אדם—"The Law speaks in accordance with the language of men." The exact significance of this principle, and the limits of its application, have been the subject of very much difference of opinion. But upon the assignation of these limits depends, to some extent, the correct estimate of the views of the Rabbis on the whole question of Inspiration. This principle is, *e.g.*, the lineal ancestor of the modern assertion that the Bible is not a Science text-book. It has been used to explain the supposed presence in the Bible, without negativing its Divine authorship, of passages which Mr. Page Hopps describes as "neither eloquent, nor beautiful, nor pure, nor edifying, nor accurate." It has been, more allowably, seized upon to explain the Biblical use of the parable as a means of enforcing moral truths. And it was by the Rabbis themselves applied to explain the Biblical anthropomorphisms; that they would never have countenanced its application to some of the other suggested objects will appear a little further on.

But if the oral traditions failed to elucidate the whole of the Sacred Text, in what sense could they, together with the latter, constitute the *whole* Word of God? To this I may briefly answer that, though the notion of a necessary addition or supplement to the *written* Law was as obviously foreign to the Rabbinical conception as the possibility of the abrogation of its permanent precepts, the same all-sufficient confidence in the finality of the *oral law*, as handed down by tradition,* was by no means felt. The traditions did not always suffice to explain the difficulties of the text. This insufficiency was probably ascribed more to the carelessness of the recipients of the traditions in later times than to a defect in the traditions themselves; and when the Talmudists, despairing of their own unaided efforts, relied on the future assistance of inspired teachers, the latter were regarded in the light of restorers of what Israel had possessed and lost, rather than of messengers of an entirely new revelation. This reliance is usually expressed in the Talmud by the puzzling word תיקו, a term that has been most ingeniously explained as formed (according to a not uncommon method) from the initial letters of a sentence meaning "The Tishbite will resolve difficulties and perplexities." The Tishbite is, of course, Elijah (1 Kings xvii. 1). Now, whether this conjectural etymology of תיקו is correct or not, at all events the fact implied is incontestably true. The advent of the Messiah, or the period immediately preceding that consum-

---

* I allude more particularly to cases in which the Methods of Interpretation had been applied to obtain the results.

mation, was looked forward to for the settlement of disputed questions of Biblical interpretation. Malachi (iv. 4-6) is probably the basis of this supposition.

To sum up this somewhat involved discussion. The Bible in all its parts was, for the Rabbis, the Word of God. But it was not the whole of His Word. There were, besides, the oral traditions, which were the Word of God no less than the Sacred Scriptures. But beyond these two divisions the Word of God did not extend.

2. The answer to the question heading this discussion given by modern Jews must be dismissed in a brief space, and that because a definite answer is impossible. There is no single opinion on the question which could at the present day be called the Jewish opinion. Strange as it may seem, Jews enjoy a very wide latitude in the views they hold on what appear the most essential points of the faith, the reason for this being the absence of any authoritative and universally approved creed. Hence, even on this question of Inspiration, there may be seen amongst modern Jews adherents of the most opposed views.

Certainly the majority of Jews—not of English Jews perhaps—hold fast to the old conception as set forth above. An advanced section, however, known as the "Reformed Jews," contest the validity of the older assumptions, though even within this section there are some sub-divisions. First, the authenticity of the oral traditions is denied. So far as this denial is concerned, it is usual to assert that the Jews of the Reform approximate to the tenets of the Karaites. This assertion is hardly correct. The Karaites were indeed so called from their supposed affection for the written text of the Bible, which is in Rabbinic Hebrew known as קרא (*Kara*) or מקרא. The sect, however, which is mentioned neither by Josephus nor Philo, is comparatively modern, and its formation dates from the eighth century of the present era. To the Karaites the ancient views both of the Sadducees and of the Samaritans have been variously attributed, but this has been done without sufficient real knowledge of what the Karaites actually profess. There is even a doubt as to whether the Karaites accept the whole of the books of the Old Testament, or the Pentateuch only, as the Word of God. A characteristic which they have in common with the modern advanced Jews is the figurative interpretation they place upon those Biblical passages which refer to certain external observances, such as the *tephillin*. Still, as far as can be made out, the Karaites scarcely deserve the name of a distinct sect; for, though they dispute the authority of the Talmud, "their enslavement to tradition is quite as complete as that of any Talmudist could possibly be."

Whether the Jews of the Modern Reform in England, Germany, and America, call themselves Karaites or not, they have at least thrown off altogether the belief in the inspiration of the oral traditions. To most of them the Bible is still the Word of God, and to many, also, the whole of His Word. A distinction is, again, drawn between the Pentateuch and the other portions of Scripture; and the Mosaic authorship of the Pentateuch is, by one section, not regarded as a necessary tenet, nor is the Bible conceived as the entire and final revelation of God's Word. "Without denying the inspiration of the Bible,"—writes Mr. Claude Montefiore, in the *Contemporary Review*,— "it [the Reformed Judaism] can escape from the bondage and death of the letter to the liberty and life of the spirit." . . . "Orthodox Judaism, if it be consistent, must cling to the Mosaic authorship of the whole Pentateuch. It is a dogma of its faith that the whole law—perfect and immutable —was revealed by God to Moses, and written down by Moses in the form in which we now possess it. Reformed Judaism is under no such obligation. The perfection and immutability of the law contained within the Pentateuch is not a dogma which it can recognise, for it views the whole Hebrew Scriptures in a different light from orthodoxy. It denies that religion can be contained, complete and entire, within the pages of any book. It denies that any book does not possess a human as a Divine side. It rejects the theory of verbal inspiration. For the theory of verbal inspiration necessarily implies that every sentence in the Pentateuch is perfect in itself. But Reformed Judaism does not hold itself responsible for, and bound by, every utterance and every law in the Biblical Canon." I quote this passage from a recent article of a prominent member of the Reformed Judaism in England, as it well illustrates how far a writer can go and still call himself a Jew. In a portion of this passage, and more particularly in the quotation following from Holdheim, a leader of Jewish Reform in Germany, we find the writers falling back on what seems a misapplication of a principle already alluded to. "Religion," writes Holdheim, in his *Predigten*, "can only be revealed to man through man. But that which can only be given through man cannot be given perfect and complete. . . . The endless capacity for development which distinguishes the

Mosaic doctrine of God, is part of the foundations of Judaism, belongs, I would almost say, to the fundamental articles of the Jewish faith." Now there seems something wrong in this line of argument. The Bible, it is said, is the Word of God; but in so far as it was revealed through man to man, it must be imperfect. This is true. But those who employ this argument seem not to perceive that the imperfections so allowed for could only be such as are inherent to the human mind; could only be imperfections such as no man could remedy. To suppose otherwise is, indeed, to consider the Bible as wanting in that which alone could justify its claim *in any sense* to the title of the Word of God.

I must now break off, but not before saying one or two words with reference to the main contention of Rev. J. Page Hopps' article. I see no reason why the most pronounced Talmudist should demur to that contention. By all means let everything that is beautiful in Man or in Nature be called, in a sense, part of the Word of God. "The heavens declare the glory of God: and the firmament showeth His handiwork. Day unto day uttereth speech, and night unto night showeth knowledge" (Psalm xix. 1, 2). Nevertheless, there may be still another sense in which the Bible is *the* Word of God. In any case, no good seems to me to result from going the lengths that Mr. Hopps would appear inclined to lead us, at all events for those who still hold that there is a meaning in the term, direct Divine Inspiration. Any further remark on this point would, I fear, lead me far beyond the limits I assigned to my paper at the outset.

Article X.

By the Right Rev. WILLIAM WEATHERS, D.D.
(Bishop of Amycla, and Coadjutor of H. E. Cardinal Manning).

THIS question, which is being discussed by the various writers on this subject, is one of great importance. For if, in any sense, the Bible is the Word of God, it highly interests all to know in what sense this is true. I cannot, however, go along with some of those who have so expressed themselves as if they thought that the only important question concerning the Bible which claims our attention, is its Inspiration, the question of the Canon of Scripture being of comparatively little importance. How any one who holds the Bible to be the sole rule of faith can speak thus is to me an enigma. For of what practical use would it be to establish the fact of the Inspiration of the Bible, if we had no means of ascertaining what books belonged to the Bible? The two questions, viz., the Inspiration and the Canonicity of the Bible, are both of importance, and, in a certain sense, of equal importance, because they are so far connected one with the other that they must stand or fall together. Nevertheless, they are in themselves two distinct questions, and it is with the former and not with the latter that we have here to deal.

In what sense, then, is the Bible to be regarded as the Word of God?

This phrase, "the Word of God," may be taken in two different senses. It may be taken, in a stricter sense, to express those revelations or commands which come immediately from God. It is in this sense that the sacred Scripture itself uses the phrase. Or it may be taken in a wider signification, so as to comprehend whatever is written by men under the impulse of the Divine Spirit. In this latter sense the whole Bible may be truly called the Word of God, provided only that all that is therein contained has been set down under the Inspiration of the Divine Spirit. The Catholic Church holds this to be true. Her teaching on this point does not fall short of the highest doctrine maintained by any of your writers. The Council of Trent (Sess. IV. decretum de Canon Scriptur) declares God to be the author of the books of the Old and of the New Testament. It numerates those books which it recognises as sacred and canonical, including all the parts of them which have been commonly read in the Church, and which are found in the Latin Vulgate, which is declared to be an authentic version of the sacred Scriptures.

A word or two may be allowed for the purpose of explaining what is meant by this declaration of the Council as to the authenticity of the Vulgate. The word "authentic," when applied to an original document, means that the document has in all its parts the sanction of the author. When applied to a copy or a translation, it means that it agrees, in all that is essential, with the original. It is as a copy or version of the Scriptures that the Vulgate is declared to be authentic. The Council did not mean by this declaration that the Vulgate translation was the work of inspired men. It did not institute any comparison between the Vulgate and the original text, such as it exists at the present day in the Hebrew, Chaldaic, or Greek copies which have come down to us—so that they retain the same authority which they had before. Neither did the Council mean that the Vulgate was free from all errors, since it recommended the Holy See to cause a new and revised edition to be brought out. What the Council did mean by this declaration was, that the Vulgate was to be held, in substance, a faithful representation of the original text. As such it commanded that it should

M

be read in the services of the Church, and used for all the purposes for which the sacred Scriptures were given.

Following up this decree of the Council of Trent, declaring all the books of the Old and New Testament to be sacred and canonical, the Vatican Council explains more fully and explicitly (Constitutio de fide, c. 2) what we are required to believe in virtue of this decree. It is not enough to hold that these books were in their origin the fruit of human industry, and were adopted by the Church, which put the seal of her approbation upon them. Neither is it sufficient to hold that they contain the truths of revelation without any admixture of error. We are required to believe something more, viz., that they have been delivered to the Church as having been written under the inspiration of the Holy Spirit, and as having God for their true author. Catholics believe, therefore, that the sacred Scriptures are the Word of God, not merely that they contain His word. One of your writers (the Rev. Stanley Leathes) has said well, that "to affirm of the Bible that it contains the word of God, in contradistinction to its being the Word of God, is very nearly tantamount to affirming that we have no actual Word of God, at least, such as all may reasonably acknowledge, unless, in addition to saying the Bible contains the word of God, we go on to say also in what way we may determine what is or is not the Word of God."

Catholics, believing that the sacred Scriptures are the Word of God, believe also that *all they contain is infallibly true.* For can God speak that which is false? They believe more than this. Whatever a General Council decrees they hold to be infallibly true, because of the promise of our Lord to the Church that His Spirit should abide with her for ever, teaching her all truth. Yet Catholics never think of identifying the decrees of a Council with the words of sacred Scripture. What, then, is the difference between the two? The decrees of the Church's Councils are drawn up by men who are not inspired, though preserved, by the assistance of the Divine Spirit, from falling into error; whereas the sacred Scriptures are written by inspired men. "For all Scripture is given by inspiration of God" (2 Tim. iii.).

One of your writers has said, "One cannot believe that it required any very high degree of inspiration to write the Book of Ruth. Perhaps not so much was needed as for the writing of the 'Pilgrim's Progress' or the 'Christian Year.'" To me this seems nothing less than setting up human reason in judgment upon the Word of God. But my object in quoting these words is to direct attention to the fact which underlies them, and which sufficiently accounts for their being spoken. The writer—he does not stand alone in the views which he here expresses—confesses the sacred Scriptures to be truly given by inspiration of God, but takes this word "inspiration" not in that definite sense in which theological writers use it, but as being little more than a figure of speech. Just as people call Milton an inspired poet, meaning that he was inspired by his own genius, or call Pitt an inspired statesman, meaning that he was beyond all others directed by a far-seeing political sagacity, so does he call Bunyan and Keble inspired religious writers, in the sense that they discoursed in no ordinary way upon the lofty themes to which they devoted their pen. But to speak of the sacred Scriptures as inspired in this sense of the word is the same thing as to deny the inspiration of the Scriptures altogether. In what sense, then, do we use the word inspiration when applied to the writers of the sacred Scriptures? An illustration will help us to understand better the matter we are here considering.

A minister wishes to send a despatch to some agent abroad. He makes known to his secretary, whose services he calls into requisition, what it is he desires to say. He leaves it to his secretary to draw up the despatch in his own way, but takes care to see that the wording accurately represents his own meaning. Now here the minister is the real author of the despatch which has been prepared. Nevertheless, the secretary, in drawing it up in strict conformity with the instructions given to him, has not been simply a passive instrument in the hands of his chief, but has placed at his disposal the services of a free agent.

Now in some way analogous to this God has vouchsafed to communicate His Word to us by the writing of inspired men. He has commissioned them to fulfil the office before Him of scribe or secretary. He has imparted to them, in such way as He judged fit, a knowledge of the facts He desired to be put on record, a knowledge of the truths of revelation and of the doctrinal and moral instructions He wished to be committed to writing. In the execution of the task assigned to them, of putting down in writing what He had made known to them, He may have acted with them in the same manner as He did with the prophets who delivered their message by word of mouth, that is to say, He may have left them to the use of their natural faculties, furnishing to them at the same time the assistance of His Divine Spirit, so as to guard them from either adding to, or detracting from, the fulness and integrity of His Word.

Now this immediate action of God upon man— first, appointing him to act as a sacred amanuensis or scribe; second, instructing him what he is to say; and third, so directing him in the execution of the task assigned as to secure exact fulfilment— is what we mean by Divine Inspiration.

But what ground have we for affirming that the Inspiration vouchsafed to the writers of the sacred books included as much as is here stated? Because, as nothing more than this would be required, so nothing less than this would be sufficient to warrant our affirming God to be the author of these books. If these books had been put together by mere human industry, and had afterwards been declared by competent authority to contain the revelation of God free from all error, they might have been called, in a certain sense, the Word of God, but they could not be called the Inspired Word of God, much less could they be said to have God for their author. Yet the Apostle tells us that *all* Scripture is the Inspired Word of God (2 Tim. ii.), and the Church has, by what we believe to be the infallible definitions of her Councils, declared that God Himself is the author of the books both of the Old and the New Testaments.

After considering what is included in the theory of Inspiration as held by Catholics, it may be well to consider what might seem to be implied therein, but in reality is not. From the fact of the sacred writers being inspired it does not necessarily follow that they were themselves conscious they were writing under the influence of the Divine Spirit. Divine grace may move the will of man, and with his co-operation produce the fruit of justification—which is a Divine work—without man being conscious of the action of grace upon his soul. So, in like manner, the gift of Inspiration may descend upon a man and work its effects in him, without making its presence known. The Spirit breatheth where He will. We have, as a matter of fact, good reason for believing that in many, if not most cases, the sacred writers did know they were acting under the Divine guidance. To Jeremiah it was said (xxx. 2), "Write thee all the words that I have spoken to thee in a book." In Habakkuk we read (ii. 2), "The Lord answered me, and said, Write the vision and make it plain upon tablets." Many such citations might be given. On the other hand, we have ground in some cases for believing that the writers, though inspired, had not themselves any knowledge of the fact. We are told that St. Mark, yielding to the entreaty of the Christians at Rome, wrote his Gospel previous to his departure for Alexandria. Again St. Luke, in the opening verses of his Gospel, assigns as the motive of his writing the fact of his possessing better opportunities than others of furnishing an exact record of the events which had taken place. The above-named circumstances furnish, it is true, no ground whatever for doubting that these Evangelists were inspired. God might as easily, so to speak, make use of the solicitations of friends to induce the one to undertake the task He had assigned to him, as He might have furnished the other with those available sources of information which he speaks of, to the end he might be duly fitted for the work of an Evangelist. Nevertheless, the circumstances may leave room to doubt whether the Evangelists themselves were conscious, at the time, of their possessing the gift of Inspiration. We have another example in the case of the writer of the Second Book of the Machabees (xv. 39). And it seems certain that Caiaphas, when he uttered the words, " It is expedient for you that one man should die for the people, and that the whole nation perish not," did not know that he was inspired to speak thus. Yet, as we read, he did not speak these words of himself, but, being the High Priest that year, he uttered a prophecy.

Again, from the fact of the sacred writers being inspired, it does not follow that there is not a human element as well as a Divine in their writings. They were men having their own natural gifts, differing from one another in their previous education, with a more or less extensive vocabulary of words. Now God did not by the gift of inspiration change their nature, but He consecrated it to His service. Hence the writers have left the impress of their individual character upon their writings. Thus the prophet Amos, who was called when following the cattle, uses—as we are told by those who are familiar with the Hebrew text—a rustic simplicity of style very unlike the refined and elevated language of the royal prophet Isaiah. Thus St. Luke, when describing the different diseases cured by our Lord, makes use of medical terms which we do not meet with in the accounts given by the other Evangelists. I cannot, however, agree with those who, applying to the present case the maxim *humanum est errare*, contend that these writers, being in themselves fallible, cannot be supposed to have been made by the gift of Inspiration exempt from error. To argue thus is to lose sight of the direct and immediate action of God which enters into our idea of Inspiration.

If it be true, however, that there is no substantial difference between what is held by Catholics, and what is held by a large class of Protestants, as regards the theory of Inspiration, it is not so as regards the proofs of Inspiration, *i.e.*, the ground upon which we hold the Bible to be inspired. The reasons given by your writers—not excepting the elaborate argument contained in the able paper of the Rev. Stanley Leathes, to which I shall make special reference—seem to me quite inadequate to establish the fact of the Inspiration of the Bible.

I admit that the Rev. Professor gives one argument amply sufficient to prove the Inspiration of the Old Testament. As he truly says : " The New Testament, beyond all question, claims and assumes that honour for the Old." It is well known what great reverence the Jews had for their sacred books, which they regarded as Divine. Now our blessed Lord did not condemn this belief of theirs. On the contrary, by appealing as He did to the Scriptures as an unimpeachable authority, He sanctioned and confirmed that belief. If, then, the writings of the New Testament be admitted to be genuine —and this much is here assumed—they prove that our blessed Lord accepted the books of the Old

Testament as inspired. And this is an argument abundantly sufficient to establish the Inspiration of the Old Testament. It is an argument, however, which obliges us to accept as inspired, not merely those sacred books which were written in Hebrew, and are contained in the Canon of Esdras, but also the books written later in Chaldaic or Greek, and inserted in the Septuagint Version. Why do I say so? As I cannot enter into any detailed proof of a matter which relates to the canonicity, rather than the inspiration of the Scriptures, suffice it to say, that out of 350 citations from the Old Testament which occur in the New, 300 are taken from the Septuagint Version (Hurter, Theol: Compend; Tract 2, Thesis 35); and that there are many references in the New Testament to passages contained in books which belong, not to the Hebraic, but to the Septuagint canon (cf. Tob. iv. 6; Matt. vii. 12; 2 Mach. vi. 19; Heb. ix. 35; Ecclus. xxx. 4.; 2 Cor. ix. 7).

We will pass now to the New Testament. We have here no Scripture testimony affirming the Inspiration of any part of it beyond the indirect testimony to that effect which St. Peter bears to the Epistles of St. Paul (2 Peter iii. 16). How then can we prove the writings of the New Testament to be the Inspired Word of God?

The principal argument brought forward by the Rev. Stanley Leathes, for the purpose of proving both the Old and the New Testament to be inspired, is founded on what is called the organic unity of the Bible. The argument may be stated thus:—The Bible is an organic whole. The character of the Bible as a whole must be judged by the character of its principal parts. Now these principal parts—the sublime moral lessons which are inculcated, the revelations and prophecies which are contained—are the Inspired Word of God. Therefore the Bible, taken as a whole and with all its parts, must be recognised as the Inspired Word of God. But let me ask what Bible are we here speaking of? Is the Catholic Bible, with its Book of Machabees, bearing testimony to the doctrine of Purgatory, to be recognised as an organic whole, and as the Inspired Word of God? "No!" our opponents will exclaim. "You have admitted into your Bible many books which ought not to find any place there." But if Catholics and Protestants thus differ from each other, and if Protestants abroad differ amongst themselves, as to what books properly belong to the Bible, is it not manifest that this argument is valueless to prove that any book or any part thereof is to be accounted as inspired because it is contained in the Bible, until it has first been established upon independent ground that the said book, with all its parts, is entitled to be admitted into the Bible? Neither can any one, in default of direct evidence of the inspiration of the several books of Scripture, assume those books to be canonical which are accepted as such by all the different churches, so long as his principles oblige him to deny the validity of the grounds upon which they are accepted by others as such.

This first argument, therefore, is fallacious. It cannot prove that the Bible is inspired until it be first shown that the books in the Bible have a right to be there because they belong to the canonical Scriptures. What other argument is adduced then in proof of the inspiration of the books of Scripture? The same writer quotes the words of St. Paul to the Thessalonians (1 Thess. ii. 13): "We thank God because, when you received the word of God which you heard of us, you received it not as the word of man, but, as it is in truth, the word of God, which effectually worketh also in you who believe." What the writer says upon this passage resolves itself into two arguments—one being based upon the efficacy of the Divine word in the case of those who believe, the other being founded upon the recognition on the part of the Thessalonians of the Divine authority of St. Paul's teaching.

Our blessed Lord said to His Apostles, " Preach the Gospel to every creature. He that believeth and is baptized shall be saved." The Apostle tells the Thessalonians, in like manner, that the Gospel which he preached to them—the Gospel is called in many places of Scripture the Word of God —worketh effectually in those who believe. The Apostle speaks here of preaching, but I do not dispute the justice of the inference that the same evangelical truths, whether they be heard or whether they be read, will in the one case, no less than in the other, work effectually in the heart of believers. But surely the writer would not have us infer from this that the book containing any such truths must in all its parts be regarded as inspired—unless, indeed, the book in all its parts should have been written by an Apostle.

This, then, is the second argument. It is based upon the authority due to the teaching of an Apostle, whether it be delivered by word of mouth or in writing. I am far from denying the force of this argument. Among those who have dwelt most strongly on this argument is Michaelis, a name held in great repute amongst Protestants. He contends, in his Introduction to the New Testament, that this is the proper ground upon which the Inspiration of the New Testament should be rested. But then he candidly admits that this argument does not meet the whole case, that the Inspiration of the Gospels of St. Mark and St. Luke can neither be maintained on this ground, nor yet upon that of ancient documents that have come down to us, but only upon the authority of the Church's testimony.

Bishop Wordsworth, one of your writers tell us, goes further. He admits that the sacred Scriptures as a whole can be received upon no other authority but that of the testimony of the primitive Church, but contends that this testimony is conclusive against the Church of Rome. I have not myself read his book. But seeing that all the Churches of the East, both those which are in communion with the Holy See and those which are not, agree together upon this point, that the testimony of the early Church obliges them to receive the same canon as the Church of Rome, it is not easy to understand how Bishop Wordsworth, with the same evidence before him, arrives at a conclusion opposed to the judgment of the Church, both East and West.

It is quite true that, when the times of persecution were over, a certain diversity of opinion was found to exist in different parts of the Church concerning some of the inspired writings. The cause of this divergence is not far to seek, but I abstain from entering upon an explanation which would take me away from the subject I am engaged upon. I wish only to point out how this division in the Church did not, as with other religious bodies, lead to any rupture, but was speedily closed. This was because all were agreed upon the one principle which applied to the solution of doubts, as in other matters relating to doctrine, so in this relating to the books which were to be received as inspired. And what was that principle? St. Paul had said to Timothy, whom he had appointed Bishop of Ephesus, "The things which thou hast heard from me before many witnesses, the same commend to faithful men who shall be fit to teach others also" (2 Tim. ii.). The Church acted then, as she has acted ever since, in accordance with this precept given by the Apostle. She set herself to trace out, through the testimony of her Bishops and Clergy, what was the Apostolic tradition handed down by the several Churches on this important question. Could it be supposed that they—the Bishops and Clergy of the different Churches—who had been willing to lay down their lives rather than deliver up the sacred writings into the hands of the persecutors, were altogether ignorant from what source they had received the precious deposit which they possessed? When, therefore, the Church, to whom Christ had promised the assistance of His Divine Spirit, had satisfied herself what traditions were proved to be genuine and authentic, she published, in the acts of her approved Councils,—Hippo, A.D. 393, Carthage, A.D. 397—the catalogue of those sacred books which she recognised then as canonical, and has continued ever since to recognise as such.

Now this method of proceeding, which I have said was in accordance with the rule laid down by the Apostle, was the most reasonable, nay, the only possible method which the Church could have adopted. I say the most reasonable method. By what other means but that of the authoritative testimony of the Church could the unlearned of that or of any other age be brought to know what books are the Inspired Word of God? By what other means but this can the learned be brought— would to God that all might be brought—to be of one mind on this vital question? I say the only possible method. For inspiration is a Divine operation, not necessarily known to the mind that is acted upon, hidden from all but those to whom God reveals it, either directly, by His own mouth, as when He spoke to St. John (Rev. i. 19), "Write, therefore, the things which thou hast seen," or indirectly, through the voice of others whom He has commissioned to speak in His name, viz., the Apostles and those to whom the Apostles have delivered the knowledge of the mysteries of God, that is, the Pastors of the Church, to whom He has said, He that heareth you heareth me (Luke x. 16). The only satisfactory proof that can, then, be given of the Inspiration of sacred Scripture is the testimony of God, and the way by which we, to whom God has made no direct personal revelation on the subject, come to this knowledge, is by the testimony of the Church, which He has commanded us to hear. St. Augustine, who was no sceptic, but a deep Christian thinker and a Doctor of the Church, recognised so clearly this truth that he hesitated not to say, "I would not believe the Gospel unless the authority of the Church moved me thereto" (Cont. Ep. Fund, c. 5).

Within what limits is the Bible to be regarded as the Word of God?

I. Admitting the Bible to be the Word of God, are we required to believe in its verbal inspiration? This question is not one of so much consequence as might at first be imagined, because it cannot be understood to refer to any version of the sacred Scriptures, but only to the original text, and such existing copies as can be ascertained to be authentic. Catholics are under no sort of obligation to believe that inspiration extends to the words of Holy Scripture as well as to the subject matter which is therein contained. The following arguments seem to tell against admitting the verbal inspiration of the Scriptures except in certain particular parts.

1. The Eighteenth Psalm, written by David, is inserted in 2 Samuel xxii. as well as in the Book of Psalms. The substance is in both cases the same, but the wording differs considerably. St. Augustine takes occasion from this to deprecate insisting needlessly upon the use of identical terms in matters of religion, so long as the identity of doctrine is maintained.

2. The Apostles, in citing Holy Scripture, give usually the substance, not the exact words of the text to which they refer.

3. In like manner, the discourses of our Blessed Lord are not reproduced by the Evangelists precisely in the same form. Thus, *e.g.*, in the Institution of the Sacrament of the Blessed Eucharist at the last supper, as set forth by three Evangelists

and by St. Paul, there is a perfect unity in the substance of the doctrine, joined with a certain diversity in the language of its exposition. We do not lose thereby. On the contrary, each record adds something to our knowledge of that great mystery.

Although, then, we reject verbal inspiration, it is still imperative upon us to lay great stress upon all the words of sacred Scripture, because, the matter being inspired of which the words are the accurate exponents, it is by weighing well their meaning and their force that we arrive at a deeper sense of the truths they set forth.

II. Admitting the Bible to be the Inspired Word of God, are we bound in consequence, absolutely and unconditionally, to receive the whole matter contained in the Bible, irrespectively of whether it relates to religion, or to history and science?

This question opens up a large subject, which would require to be treated at too great length for any justice to be done to it here. I will offer a few remarks only in reply.

If we recognise that God is in a true sense the author of the books of the Old and New Testament, it is clear that we are bound to receive, with implicit faith, whatever those books teach on the subject of religion and morality,—the guidance of men in these matters being the very end for which those books were given under the inspiration of the Holy Ghost. " But what of the dark and cruel things which were attributed to God or done at His instigation?" I may be in error, but I understand the Rev. J. Page Hopps here to refer to such things recorded in the Bible, as the command given to the Israelites to exterminate the inhabitants of the land of Canaan. But why was this command given? "The land," it is written, "is defiled. Therefore do I visit the iniquity thereof upon it; and the land itself vomiteth out its inhabitants" (Lev. xviii.). As God punished a sinful race by the Deluge, and the corrupt cities of the plain by fire from heaven, so did He destroy the Canaanites by the sword, because of their wickedness. And He gave the Israelites the charge of carrying out the sentence, that they themselves might beware, lest, falling into the same sins, they should draw down upon themselves a like judgment. If the innocent were in all these cases involved with the guilty in one common punishment, we must bear in mind that God will hereafter judge men separately, and allot to each one a just reward. But here in this life He judges empires, He judges nations, as such, when the voice of their guilt reaches the heavens.

Lastly, we have to consider those things which are contained in the Bible, which do not relate to religion, but belong to the department of history or science. Are we, in consequence of our believing the Bible to be inspired, compelled to let these things go also unchallenged, or are we free to reject them on the ground that the Bible was not intended to teach science or history? First let me ask, however, whether it can be admitted that these things contained in the Bible have no relation to religion? If we hold that the Bible not merely contains, but is, the Word of God, and if we say that these things not merely have no connection with religion, but are absolutely false, how have they got into the Bible at all, since it is clear that they are in no sense the Word of God? It is intelligible enough how one who holds that the Bible contains the Word of God may hold, at the same time, that there are errors in the Bible. But how he who holds that the Bible is the Word of God can say the same, is to me a mystery. I know that there are Catholics who have maintained this doctrine, that there are errors in the sacred books, though not such as touch faith or morals, and they maintain this because they say the Church has never defined that there are no errors in the inspired volume. I admit the Church has never expressly defined this point. But she has laid down the premisses as of faith from which no other conclusion can be legitimately drawn, but that there is nothing false in the sacred Scriptures. This of course is said of the original text of the Divine Word. It is admitted that there are errors in all the existing copies of the originals, as well as in the different versions which have been made from them. The Council of Trent declared that in the Vulgate we have a translation which is in substance the same as the original. Writing to St. Jerome, St. Augustine (Ep. lxxxii. 3) shows the great respect he had for the Scriptures. "I confess," he says, "that I render to no other book the honour and reverence I pay to the canonical Scripture, believing firmly that none of the writers to these books have fallen into any error. If in these writings I come across anything which seems to me at variance with the truth, I have no doubt but that either my copy is faulty, or the translator has erred, or I mistake his meaning."

But I may be told that this is an exploded

theory, that all who have regard to the state of modern science are compelled to lay down qualifications and to make reserves which are a virtual surrender of the infallibility of the Bible. What then are these errors, scientific or otherwise, which have been proved to exist in the Bible ? Because it must be admitted that if errors have been proved, the belief in the infallibility of the Bible is at an end. Now I admit that it is not impossible for science to do what it has done before, viz., prove that our interpretation of many things in Scripture is false. St. Augustine warned Catholics in his day not to put forth their private interpretation of facts related in the Bible as if it were authentic, because when learned men amongst unbelievers hear that asserted on the authority of the Bible, which they know to be false, they will naturally say, If the Bible is shown to be untrustworthy in those lesser things, where it can be tested, how can credit be given to it in higher things, where verification is impossible ? But it is one thing to prove our interpretation of the Bible to be erroneous, and another thing to prove the Bible itself to be in error.

The assertion on the part of men of science that they have disproved the Bible, has been repeated over and over again; but the men of science of each succeeding age have uniformly disavowed the accepted proofs brought forward in earlier times, and we may rest assured that the twentieth century will pronounce a similar verdict upon the so-called scientific proofs of the nineteenth century.

Article XI.

By the Venerable Archdeacon Farrar, D.D.

THE question—In what sense is the Bible regarded as the Word of God?—naturally seems to invite a purely historical treatment. It might be answered by a catalogue of the opinions maintained in different ages respecting the nature and limits of "Inspiration," so far as the use of that term (of which the Catholic Church has never attempted or accepted any accurate definition) is supposed to imply that the Bible *is* "the Word of God." The particular formulation of the question would seem to call for a chapter in the History of Dogmas.

It has not, however, been so treated by the writers whose views are given in the previous pages. One and all of them—Anglican Professor, Presbyterian, Congregationalist, Unitarian, Swedenborgian, Wesleyan, Jew, and Roman Catholic—have given their own personal views, or those of the religious body to which they belong. It is evident that they have all understood the thesis in the sense preferred by Mr. Page Hopps—"In what sense, and within what limits, *is* the Bible the Word of God?"

1. Professor Stanley Leathes begins at once by disparaging the statement that the Bible "*contains*" the Word of God, and asserting that it *is* the Word of God. His paper is apparently an argument that the terms "Bible" and "Word of God" are to be regarded as co-extensive.

2. Dr. Cairns, closely agreeing with Dr. Leathes, furnishes additional arguments and illustrations in support of the same view.

3. The Rev. A. Mackennal, while he claims for the Bible an unique place in literature, and agrees with the statements of the preceding writers that it is "an organic whole" and a Divine Book, enforces the fact that neither the Scriptures as a whole, nor any separate books of Scripture, put forward any claim to be "the Word of God." He says that, though the phrase "Word of God" occurs three or four hundred times in the Old Testament, and a hundred times in the New, it is not, in a single instance, applied to Scripture itself. He thinks that the very distinction which Dr. Leathes denies, between the Bible and some of its contents, is grounded on Scripture itself. His paper is mainly occupied with definitions of the senses in which the phrase "Word of God" is used

in the Bible; and as a result of his inquiry, he holds that in the Old Testament it should be confined to special revelations, and in the New to Christ alone. He says that for many years he has hesitated to describe Scripture by a term which he regards as unauthorised, and that his hesitation is increased rather than abated by the arguments of Dr. Leathes and Dr. Cairns. It is difficult to see what the previous writers exactly mean, but Mr. Mackennal's meaning is very clear. "The attempt," he says, "to attach a name of special sanctity to all the contents of the Bible, ends in the degradation of that name itself."

4. Mr. Page Hopps, while agreeing with Mr. Mackennal in his rejection of the term "Word of God" as applied to all Scripture, goes further still. He, as a Unitarian, cannot even accept the view that the Bible is "the authorised record of the way in which God communicated His will to man." He thinks that many even of the utterances expressly attributed to "the Word of the Lord," contain "all kinds of trivialities and not a few absurdities." Many readers may be startled by these expressions, and it is not my object here to examine them. Mr. Page Hopps might, however, argue that they are implied by even the most orthodox Roman Catholic commentators, who only get over such

apparent difficulties by the aid of allegory and the mystic sense. Even such a commentator as Pagninus says, "Quic quid in sermone divino *neque ad piorum honestatem neque ad fidei veritatem proprie referri potest*, figuratum esse cognoscas." Even so orthodox a scholar as Flacius Illyricus speaks of places where the grammatical sense " pugnat cum sana doctrinâ vel adversatur bonis moribus." He says that the Bible is only the Word of God " as all created things are words of His," and denies that Inspiration is either supernatural or miraculous. He would extend the use of the term to what is called secular literature, and hold that King Alfred and Luther and Tyndale spoke the word of the Lord as well as the Hebrew prophets. In support of these opinions he points out that not only does the Bible evince no infallibility in scientific matters, but that it contains " much which is neither eloquent, nor beautiful, nor pure, nor edifying, nor accurate ; " that we find in it " varying standards of morality ; " and that the Revelation which it contains has been understood in as many different manners as there are different sects in the Christian Church.

5. Mr. W. Crosby Barlow says that the Bible contains a revelation, but that a revelation may be translucent, or obscure, or mingled ; and that even

such a "translucent" revelation as the Pauline Epistles, presupposed for its right apprehension an anterior revelation which is more or less obscure. Since even the "translucent" revelation is conditioned by the writer's possibilities as well as by the reader's illuminated receptivity, it cannot, under such limitations, be regarded as either perfect or final. He, as a Swedenborgian, does not, therefore, accept, without large qualification, the view that "The Bible is the Word of God," and says that that Word is not a written book, but is "the presence among men of the Spirit of Jehovah."

6. Professor Olver, in writing from a Wesleyan standpoint, avers, in answer to Mr. Mackennal, that "the Word of God" is a phrase which, in the New Testament, is not confined to special utterances, and that since the Apostles spoke of preaching the Word, "the usage of the New Testament justifies the custom of calling the Bible 'the Word of God.'" He proceeds to argue that "the authority of Holy Scripture is inseparable from that of the truth of Christianity." He, therefore, founds the authority of the New Testament on the Incarnation, and that of the Old on the assertion that Jesus claimed for it the authorship of the Holy Spirit. He admits that by the Bible we

must mean the original documents; he would not absolutely confine Inspiration to the sacred writers; and he maintains that neither difficulties, nor differing interpretations, nor the absence of a perfected theology, can disprove that "the Holy Scriptures are the authorised message of God's grace to man."

7. Some readers might, I think, fairly complain that of the preceding papers the three which appear to maintain the current view of the Bible as being throughout supernaturally infallible and inspired, are somewhat vague, so far as any close, definite, or fearless handling of the subject is concerned. Neither Dr. Leathes, Dr. Cairns, nor Professor Olver contribute a single element to any categorical answer of the question honestly put by the perplexed inquirer, "Is the phrase 'the Word of God' to be applied to the Bible *rigidly* or *generally?* in a strict or in a popular sense? in a sense which applies to it as a composite whole, or (as Dean Burgon says) to every chapter, verse, word and letter of it?" They seem to be fighting for a mere phrase which, after all, they are obliged to limit and modify and explain away, till it means nothing in particular. No such complaint attaches to the other three papers, whether they command our assent or not; least of all does it apply to the paper of the Rev. E. White,

which is the clearest, the ablest, and the most powerful of the whole series. He would argue the question, as an Independent, not *a priori*—beginning with "the old ecclesiastical theory of Inspiration," but *a posteriori*, studying the Scriptures apart from such traditional theories. Stating, only to repudiate, the common ecclesiastical idea of the Bible—that it is one Book which "from Genesis to Revelation is alike and equally the Word of God;" he shows—

(1) That in the first age of Christianity there is no trace of any conception of "the Bible" or "the New Testament" as one all-inspired Book, produced by a homogeneous theopneustic process.

(2) That the Canon was slowly formed by ecclesiastical opinion, not resting on inspired authority.

(3) That the books of the Bible must be read and studied as distinct treatises; and that, so studied, they will at once teach us the absurdity of claiming for their production more than they each claim for themselves, or of asserting for all alike some uniform measure and quality of "Inspiration."

Mr. White regards the notion of a homogeneous infallibility running throughout the Bible as a pernicious delusion, and appeals to St. Luke's preface as showing that the Evangelists only claim to be truthful witnesses. He says that the Scripture notion of Revelation is a union of three elements—"facts" in the world of phenomena; "God-given ideas" in the world of thought; and a verifying faculty bestowed on the divinely-touched soul. For his further remarks I must refer to his paper. I agree with it more nearly than with any of the others, and in various works I have already urged, almost in the same words, some of the very same considerations about the Bible regarded as a *progressive* Revelation, and about the fearful evils which have resulted from the abuse of mechanical theories of a continuous verbal infallibility.

8. The paper of Professor Abrahams is chiefly interesting as a proof that even among the Jews, who have in many ages treated the very letters of Scripture with an adoration hardly distinguishable from fetish-worship, there are now, and for centuries have been, wide differences of opinion on the subject of Inspiration. The common Jewish opinion, however, is, that every part of the Bible was equally inspired; and that the proof of its inspiration is an inspired tradition, and that its traditional interpretation is also inspired. To the orthodox Jew, therefore, not the Bible only, but also the oral tradition, is "the Word of God"—the only limitations being those which are inevitably

incident to human language, according to the maxim that "the Law speaks in the tongue of the children of men." And yet, after all this elaborate endeavour to protect a particular dogma concerning Scripture, the hedges of orthodoxy have been so frequently broken down, that, at the present day, "there is no single opinion on the question which can be called the Jewish opinion."

9. Lastly comes the Bishop of Amycla. He says that the Bible may be called the Word of God in the sense that "It was written by men under the inpulse of the Holy Spirit," and "that all that is therein contained has been set down under the imspiration of the Divine Spirit." He explains that by "the Bible" the Council of Trent means specifically the Latin Vulgate, including the Apocrypha, and that "God" is the "author" of the Bible (Apocrypha and all), and that all which it contains is infallibly true. The three proofs which he offers for this wide proposition are : (1) 2 Tim. iii. 16. (2) The fact that "as nothing more than this would be required, so nothing less than this would be sufficient." (3) That it has been asserted by the infallible definition of Councils. He adds, however, (i.) that the sacred writers were not necessarily conscious of their own Inspiration ; (ii.) that there is a human as well as a Divine

element in their writings. Reverting to the question of proof, he declares the arguments of the previous writers, who have maintained that "the Bible is the Word of God," are quite inadequate to establish the Inspiration of the Bible. He thinks that the Inspiration of the Old Testament is indeed established by the New, including in the term Old Testament both the Aprocrypha and the Septuagint Version. But, apart from "St. Peter's indirect testimony to the Epistles of St. Paul" (2 Peter iii. 16), there is no such proof for the New Testament. He thinks that the "organic whole" argument of Dr. Leathes falls to the ground, because it has nothing to say to the question of canonicity. He points out that St. Paul's appeal to the effectual working of the Word of God, is something widely different from a dogmatic declaration that all parts of the New Testament are equally inspired. He agrees with Bishop Wordsworth in saying, that the Scriptures as a whole can only be received on the testimony of the Primitive Church; in accordance with which view he appeals to the Council of Hippo, A.D. 393, and the Council of Carthage, A.D. 397. Turning to limitations he sets aside as unimportant, and argues against, the doctrine of verbal Inspiration, on the grounds of the differing forms in which the

Apostles quote Scripture and the Evangelists report the words of Christ. But, in opposition (as he admits) to the opinions of some Catholics, he denies that there are any errors, even in historic or scientific matters, in the sacred books, and asserts that it is only our interpretations which have been mistaken, not the Bible itself.

I have thus endeavoured to summarise the views of each writer. If, apart from its necessary brevity, there be the least unfairness or inadequacy in the summary, they will, I know, accept my assurance that it is unintentional. Moreover, as their papers are before the reader to correct any mistaken impression which they may have left on my mind, I cannot do them any injustice. The whole series of papers—were it only from the variety of views which they express—is a highly curious and valuable contribution to our views respecting a question which has filled many volumes, but about which another century must elapse before the last word is spoken. Meanwhile, there is scarcely one of these papers which does not suggest some thought or principle which is well worthy of attention.

1. To a great extent it is clear that a question about which Christian writers differ so widely,

must be much less important than to some of the writers it appears to be. This consideration alone ought to be suggestive to those who adopt the extremer views. There is not one among them all who does not regard the Bible as a collection of books which have, as a whole, a unique and supreme claim to our study and reverence. There is not one of them who would deny that in this Book, or nowhere, we find those sovereign truths which are the rule of our faith, and the guide of our conduct. Amid such a consensus of opinion concerning the majestic superiority of the Bible to all other collections of national literature, because in it we hear most directly that still small voice, in whose accents we recognise the messages of God, the question whether or not we call the whole sixty-six books by one particular term— "the Word of God"—sinks into very secondary importance. In the first place, as Mr. Mackennal well points out, it is not a scriptural term at all; and in the next place, if it be thus applied, it becomes, in any case, so ambiguous as to be understood in very different senses. Those who appear to apply it to the Bible most extensively, and in its strictest sense, surround it with such important limitations and modifications, as to rob it of all power to connote for any practical purpose the absolute perfection, and the absolute infallibility, which should properly attach to a term so awful as "the Word of God."

2. Secondly, it is encouraging to find, amid such apparent diversities, so much substantial agreement as to the authority and preciousness of Scripture. This much, at least, results from the discussion, if in other respects it does not throw any light upon the degree, extent, or nature of that undefined and indefinite "inspiration," which theologically describes the composition of the Holy Book.

3. Thirdly, there are many incidental views in these papers in which all Christians agree. All Christians are at one with the previous writers in placing the Bible above all other books. They may learn from Mr. Mackennal that the popular use of the phrase "Word of God," is not identical with its use in the sacred writers. However much they may dissent from Mr. Page Hopps, they must admit that it is not in Scripture only that God speaks to us; and that if in another sense, yet in a very true sense, He speaks to us also by "the starry heavens above, and the moral law within;" by creation and by conscience; by the heavens which declare His glory, and the earth which utters forth His praise, so that—

"Every bird that sings,
And every flower that stars the elastic sod,
And every breath the radiant summer brings,
To the pure spirit is a word of God."

They may learn from him to appreciate the remark of Luther that "God spake" does not mean an articulate voice in the air; that "God does not reveal grammatical vocables but essential things. Thus sun and moon, Peter and Paul, thou and I, are nothing but words of God." Words of God—yes; but certainly not supernaturally infallible!

They may also learn from Mr. Hopps to make due allowance for the certainty that Scripture is not all written on the same level of uniformity, and that it contains elements of very differing values. Without being Swedenborgians, they will concede to Mr. Barlow that spiritual truths can only be spiritually discerned, and they may also be reminded of an Article of the Creed which seems often to be overlooked by those who look on Inspiration as an exhausted phenomenon—"I believe in the Holy Ghost." From the strong and manly paper of Mr. White they may learn important modifications of a hard and sterile dogma about uniform Inspiration, by grasping the composite-ness, the progressiveness, the unequal values, and the fragmentary and multifarious character of the different books, together with the complexity of the idea of Revelation. In the paper of Professor Abrahams there is at least an historic interest; and that of the Bishop of Amycla is a careful theological statement of the view held in the Church of Rome. Moreover, it results very clearly from all these papers that there is no such thing as a "Catholic," any more than there is a "Jewish," view of Inspiration. The Church has never defined either its character, its limits, or its exact application. The views of Christians differ, and no dogmatic rule has been imposed. Any one who chooses may, with perfect equanimity, and with the consent alike of Scripture, of History, and of Church tradition and authority, refuse to regard the term "Word of God" as applicable in its highest sense to all that is contained in these many books of many ages.

4. Fourthly, the two last papers furnish a singular comment on the two first. One is involuntarily reminded of the remark of Faulconbridge in "King John":—

> "O prudent discipline! from north to south,
> Austria and France shout in each other's mouth."

The Bishop of Amycla answers, and very effectually answers, Dr. Leathes. "The Bible *is* the Word of God, and it is inspired," say Dr. Leathes and Dr. Cairns. The Old Testament is the Word of God and all inspired, says Professor Abrahams; but it needs an inspired interpretation, and we can only know that it is so by an inspired oral tradition. If we ask how we are to know that the oral tradition is inspired, there is no answer. The earth rests on an elephant, and the elephant on a tortoise, and the tortoise on ——— ? The Bible, says the Bishop of Amycla, is the Word of God and all inspired; but the Bible means essentially the Vulgate, and it includes the Apocrypha. That the Old Testament is inspired, we know, he says, from the New; but this argument is, for argumentative purposes, materially weakened, if not annihilated, when the question of canonicity is set aside, and when the Romish Church claims it as being valid for the Apocrypha, no less than for our Canon. Several of the writers say that the "inspiration" of the Old Testament is certified by the New; but if only those books or parts of books which are alluded to by our Lord and the Apostles (*e.g.*, Christological passages) are thus certified, then, on the one hand, the actual amount of the Old Testament will have to be very greatly reduced; and on the other hand, there are in the New Testament demonstrable allusions to the Apocrypha, and yet Protestants reject the Apocrypha as uncanonical and uninspired. What is the value of any reference to a perfectly general remark, like that of St. Paul in 2 Tim. iii. 16, if these preceding controversialists all alike ignore (i.) that even in the Revised Version it does not state that "*all Scripture* is given by inspiration of God," but the wholly different proposition that "*every Scripture* (or '*writing*') *inspired of God* is also profitable;" and (ii.) if there be no authority accepted by all Christians alike, to decide (for instance) whether Bel and the Dragon, and the story of Susanna, belong to Scripture or not? Thus the Bishop of Amycla, while he accepts the same formulæ as the Anglican and Presbyterian and Wesleyan Professors, neither agrees with them as to what the Bible is, nor accepts as valid the proofs of inspiration which they adduce. He rejects the doctrine of verbal inspiration, and only receives the Scriptures as a whole on the authority of primitive tradition—the "primitive" tradition to which he specially refers being the decision of two Councils in the last decade of the fourth centuary after Christ, neither of which is accepted as authoritative by the English Church. Thus he rejects as valueless the Protestant proofs that "the Bible is the Word of God," and offers proofs, of which one ("primitive tradition") is valueless to them; a second (2 Tim. iii. 16) is controverted, and is in any case beside the point; and the third is a mere *a priori* assertion, which has no direct or practical bearing on the understanding of the question.

I have already said that my own views coincide in great measure with those of the Rev. E. White. I yield to no one of the previous writers in my estimate of the sacredness of Scripture. To its study and illustration I have devoted much of my life. I have not the least hesitation in speaking of it *generically* as "the Word of God" in the sense that in it, as a whole, I see a record of God's revelation, and therefore one of the most priceless boons which the mercy of God has granted to mankind. It is only when the general phrase is pressed into the superstitious—I had almost said the fetish-worshipping — dogma, that every word and letter of these sixty-six books proceeded supernaturally from God; and that the sacred writers were (to use one phrase adopted by the supporters of verbal inspiration) "not only the penmen, but the pens of the Holy Ghost," that the phrase becomes not only unintelligible, but profoundly dangerous. This post-Reformation dogma I reject as utterly untenable, the daughter of an unspiritual superstition, and the mother of a casuistical tyranny. To say that every word and sentence and letter of Scripture is Divine and supernatural, is a mechanical and useless shibboleth, nay, more, a human idol, and (constructively at least) a dreadful blasphemy. How such a proposition, unless carefully guarded, presents itself to the mind of a devout layman of genius—may be seen in the remarks of Mr. Ruskin. He calls it "a grave heresy," or "source of division," to declare "a group of books, accidentally associated, to be 'the Word of God.'" He explains and justifies his remarks in *Fors Clavigera*, xxxv., xxxvi. To mention but one large limitation which must immediately be made : the phrase, so understood, attributes to God the words of men like Judas, and Caiaphas, and the Pharisees, and the imprecations of enemies in the Book of Psalms, and the sceptical pessimism of the earlier parts of Ecclesiastes, and the cold, cruel sophisms which fill whole chapters of the Book of Job and the speeches of Rabshakeh, and the decrees of Persian kings, and much more of a similar nature. These belong indeed fitly to *the historic records of a progressive Revelation.* That Revelation is a revelation vouchsafed by God to men through the acts, the words and the lives of men themselves. The sum total of those acts and words, being liable to all human limitations, cannot be called "the Word of God" in anything approaching to the same high sense in which the title is applied to Christ. Nor can the book which records them be called by such a name in any other than a general meaning. If we are to stickle about popular phrases, it is infinitely nearer the truth to say, as our Church says, that the Bible "*contains*," than to say that in every part it "*is*," the Word of God.

I am, therefore, quite unable to agree with much that I find in the papers of Dr. Leathes, Dr. Cairns, and Prof. Olver. They appear to hold that all Scripture is, in every part of it, an immediate supernatural communication from God to man, and while they offer no proof which would stand a moment's examination, they are compelled, in order to prevent themselves from being entangled in complete absurdities, to entrench their dogma in so many hazy limitations that it no longer expresses any intelligible thing.

Dr. Leathes says, that it is unfair to argue from the wording of the Sixth Article in favour of the statement that "Holy Scripture *containeth* all things necessary to salvation," rather than that "the Bible *is* the Word of God," because when the Articles were framed the distinction had not been thought of; and he adds that Scripture is not "holy," except as being derived from God.

The first assertion is, I think, the reverse of the

fact. It seems clear that the expression "*containeth*" was not accidental, for we find it again in the Homilies: "Unto a Christian man there can be nothing more necessary . . . than the knowledge of Holy Scripture, forasmuch as *in it is contained* God's true word;" and again in the services for the ordering of priests and bishops: "Are you persuaded that the holy Scriptures *contain* sufficiently all doctrine required of necessity for eternal salvation through faith in Jesus Christ?"

Reformers like Luther and Calvin, feeling in their own souls the life of a free Spirit, dealt with Scripture in a much bolder, manlier, and truer way than either their predecessors or their successors. Luther in particular, in many passages, discriminates carefully between Scripture and the Word of God, and by no means uses the two phrases as identical.

The second assertion need not detain us long. A book may be called "holy" without in the least implying that it is either infallible or supernaturally communicated. We should call the "Imitatio Christi" a holy book, though it betrays a radical misconception as to the true following of Christ.

In point of fact, the confession of the earlier Reformers, and the spirit of their writings and practice—apart from a few popular and rhetorical expressions—accord with the formula "Scriptura *complectitur* verbum Dei;" whereas the formula "Scriptura *est* verbum Dei" belongs to the later Helvetic Confession, and to such post Reformation dogmatists as Calovius.* "Luther," says Diestel, "gives to the Word of God a narrower and wider sense than the Scripture. It is to him the expression of the Divine Will, especially on its ethico religious side." The two were first thoroughly and rigorously identified by George Major in his book "De origine et authoritate verbi Dei," 1550.

But Dr. Leathes proceeds to argue that if the Bible only *contains* the word of God there can be no absolute word of God at all, "since no two individuals agree as to the particular elements that are the word of God." It is strange that he should not notice that his own view does not in the smallest degree prevent the same result. Men have fought with each other, and burnt each other, and tortured and slandered and hated each other, and to the best of their little power they do so still, because, while they each declared the Bible to be the Word of God, they attached exclusive

---

* Dr Beard says, "It was an afterthought of less original and courageous minds to make no distinction between different parts of the Bible, to regard it all with the same dull and superstitious reverence, and to force the most reluctant facts into the mould of their belief."—*Hibbert Lectures*, p. 103.

importance to different expressions which occur in it, or interpreted the same expressions in wholly different ways. Is there no "Word of God" for Dr. Leathes, because for the Bishop of Amycla, Judith and Tobit are also "the Word of God?" Passing over the question of canonicity, which is so essential to his position, and bidding us accept our ordinary Canon as "sufficiently correct for all practical purposes," the Professor asserts that "beyond all question the New Testament claims and assumes for the Old" that it is the Word of God. That the Old Testament generally is referred to in the New as authoritative is clear, but so far from being called "the Word of God," it never once receives that designation. Our Lord did, indeed, say that "all things *written in Scripture concerning Him* should be fulfilled," and that "no jot or tittle of the Law should pass away;" yet these are sayings which differ *toto cœlo* from that dogma of plenary verbal inspiration with which they are strangely mixed up. Such a dogma may be found in the decrees of Trent and in some later Protestant Confessions, but has no place in our own standards, nor in any Catholic creed of Christendom, nor is it in the smallest degree involved in Scripture itself. And that our Lord's words had no such meaning is clear, since He set aside as null and void the greater part, if not the whole, of the Levitic legislation, criticising it even in an essential particular as a concession to human imperfection.

Now heaven and earth shall pass away, but "*the Word of the Lord* endureth for ever." Is this phrase, then, the fittest by which to describe even the poorest parts of that which in the days of the Apostles was already evanescing and waxing old and "being shaken," and which has since vanished away altogether? The Old Testament (as the New tells us) contains, among other things, "weak and beggarly ordinances;" "a yoke that neither our fathers nor we were able to bear;" "dead works;" a commandment which was "weak and unprofitable;" and, as the Old Testament itself tells us, "statutes which were not good" and "ordinances which did not profit." Is all this system of evanished and abrogated Levitism—is this burdensome and narrow sacerdotalism and ceremonialism necessitated by the backwardness of a stiffnecked people, but, as our Lord Himself declared, now to be partly supplemented and partly reversed—is it all to be identified with the most rigid interpretation of a phrase which should be so awful in its significance as "the Word of God?"

Dr. Leathes then proceeds to his argument about the "organic unity" of the Old Testament, and says that, though "it is only in certain parts that we can detect the Spirit of God as more especially present," and "not all parts are of equal value," yet it is inspired as a whole. Here, then, he is obliged to admit the verifying faculty, and the right of private judgment, which he had just practically excluded. If we are obliged to decide by our individual reason what books are, and what are not, the Word of God, and are compelled to say that the Word of God in this or that chapter is of less value than in another, then, after all, "every individual must discern for himself" what is *to us* or in any sense eternally valid, the Word of God in Scripture—a right which Dr. Leathes has just declared to be fatal to his own thesis. Can it be ever justifiable to criticise the moral and spiritual value of the "Word of God?" If the question of the sense in which the Bible "*is*" the Word of God is "not greatly affected" whether it does or does not include "Wisdom or Ecclesiasticus, and even the Book of Tobit," then it is difficult to see the practical importance of the phrase which in this sense is not scriptural, and is nowhere insisted on by the Church of God. The rigid interpretation of the formula must either require us to accept every verse of Scripture as the Word of God, and therefore as something transcendant, supernatural, and infallible, or it becomes a mere chameleon-theory—a Lesbian rule—a rule of lead which can be bent any way. Obviously no such rule could have been delivered to early Christians. Whatever may be the basis of such a dogma, it is certainly not based on Scripture itself. The churches founded by the first Christian missionaries had no New Testament at all, for not a line of it was then written. The final settlement of our Canon was a matter of three or four centuries; to multitudes of the early Christians no less than seven books—even of the New Testament—were, more or less, classed among the *Antilegomena*, as books of which the authenticity was not universally admitted, and which, therefore, they did not regard as sacred. On the other hand, many early Christians accepted the Epistle of Barnabas and the Pastor of Hermas, which we unhesitatingly reject. But to bring the question to a test. It has always been an open question whether the awful imprecations of Psalm cix. 5–18 are David's own words or the horrible curses of his enemies against which he is protesting. What possible gain is there in either case in saying that they "*are*" "the Word of God?" The last verse of Psalm cxxix. appears to express the unspeakable intensity of a burning hatred. In its place—as the fragment of a literature which contains a record of God's progressive revelations by means of the history and writings of a chosen people—it has its own profound instructiveness, by way of warning, if in no other way; but, seeing that the spirit of that utterance is in the most glaring antagonism to every lesson of love and mercy which we learn from Christianity and from the noblest parts of the Scriptures themselves, what valuable result arises from insisting that that verse, too,—or that Deborah's approval of Jael's cold-blooded murder of the sleeping suppliant to whom she had extended the sacred rites of hospitality, or that many passages which stand on a similar level, "*are*" the Word of God? Such superstitious and unscriptural modes of regarding Scripture have led men to believe in human sacrifice; in exterminating wars; in pious assassinations; in Jesuitical plots; in hideous massacres; in revolting persecutions; in sacerdotal tyranny; in doing evil that good may come; in the duty of indiscriminate witch-burning; in those thrice-accursed horrors of the Inquisition, and of orthodox violence and theological hatred which have lit the fires of religious murder, and reddened the soil of earth with innocent and noble blood.

The argument,—if argument it be,—about regarding Scripture as an "organic whole," and, therefore, as throughout a supernatural communication, seems to me to have a precisely opposite bearing from that to which Dr. Leathes applies it. Scripture "as a whole," in ordinary popular language, is the Word of God; but if the phrase which is true of the whole, *as a whole*, be perverted as though it applied equally to every part, it ceases to have any tolerable sense. The phrase it seems, even in the view of its defenders, can, after all, apply only to "the most important and crucial utterances" of Scripture, and we must judge for ourselves what those are. Dr. Leathes tries to prove that "the Old Testament *is* the Word of God" because it "*contains*" testimonies to Christ. There is clearly no logical relation between the two propositions. Neither from the fact that "it may be presumed to have the Divine sanction," nor from the fact that the special message of the Gospel works effectually in them that believe, nor from the authenticity of the New Testament narratives, can any inference be drawn in favour of rigidly accepting the phrase "The Bible *is* the Word of God," except in the sense in which it is adopted also by those who think it more honest, more accurate and more reverent, when they are using the stricter language of theology, to speak, as our Church speaks, of the Word of God *contained* in Scripture. When Dr. Leathes argues that the Acts of the Apostles cover an important period, and would not be valuable if not authentic, and when he, therefore, infers that "the author was delegated and commissioned to write it," and that, since "its ostensible author was also apparently the author of the third Gospel, it is, therefore, *reasonable to suppose* that he wrote with the highest possible sanction," and, therefore, that the Acts of the Apostles "*may well be* a treatise which not only contains, but even *is* the Word of God;" his ever-widening spiral *ergo* of inferences and presumptions remains, after all, obviously valueless for the support of a single dubious particular which a hostile critic may impugn. To use such arguments against the assaults of modern critics is like using bows and arrows against an army furnished with a park of artillery. They add absolutely nothing to the value which the Book has earned, from its intrinsic merit and truthfulness, as the narrative of the work wrought by God's Spirit in the spread of Christianity. So far from claiming a mechanical inspiration or a supernatural infallibility, St. Luke, even in his Gospel, puts forward no other claim than that of knowledge and diligence. Instead of employing this weak chain of "presumablys," "apparentlys," and "maybes," which have not a particle of demonstrative force, and which link us to an unscriptural phrase of dubious meaning and of many limitations, I should proceed in the very opposite manner. Taking one by one all of the objections which have been advanced against the credibility of the Acts, I should prove—as I have elsewhere tried to do— that in *every instance*, and in the minutest particulars, the accuracy and trustworthiness of the narrator can be triumphantly vindicated; and I should then claim the Acts as one of the sacred books of our faith, because of its unique value as setting forth examples so glorious and teachings so holy, and as containing the record of that growth of Christianity and of Christendom wherein, more clearly than in all other events, we hear the Voice of God speaking to us in the history of the world. Such a method yields us a solid and impregnable conclusion; the other method only thrusts upon us the rigid acceptance and indefinite expansion of an unauthenticated *a priori* phrase, incapable of definition and liable to deadly abuse.

Dr. Cairns follows in the steps of Dr. Leathes. Like him, he strangely sets aside the question of the Canon; he does not hold that the present text is the very Word of God; nor that the matter of the Bible was all revealed for the first time; nor that it is so the Word of God as not to be also the word of man; and he is " unable to answer a good many difficulties which beset a strict theory of Inspiration;" and he " does not think it necessary to say much about the *sense* in which the Bible *is* the Word of God : " and yet, he, too, clings to this formula, not in a *general* sense (in which it is perfectly admissible), but in some particular significance which it is very difficult to grasp. He admires and adopts the strange argument that the " organic unity" of a book (a phrase which for every practical purpose drops to pieces at a touch), if it imply inspiration *anywhere* implies it *everywhere;* just as though, in giving the epithet "inspired" (in a lower sense) to Shakespeare, we should necessarily thereby include all the worst plays, such as "Titus Andronicus" or " Pericles, Prince of Tyre ; " or feel ourselves bound to defend all the " insane wantonness " (as it has been called) of some of the scenes and poems. I cannot see the least validity in this " organic whole" argument. The " success" of the Bible cannot possibly prove that the *whole* of the Bible, in every verse, is supernaturally any more than it is verbally inspired. The very word "inspired" is of very little theological value, until it has been authentic-

ally or authoritatively defined. In point of fact,
it does not necessarily connote an abnormal or
discontinuous, still less an universal and supernatural infallibility. It occurs five times in our
own Prayer Book, and in every single instance it
is used of the present, not of the past; of the
natural and continuous, not of the finished and
unrenewable influences of the Holy Spirit of God.
We, too, pray for inspiration—surely not without
the belief that we shall receive it. Is our inspiration a miracle in the sense that is an exceptional
work of God within us? Does it prevent us from
intellectual error or moral weakness? Does it
make all we say infallible? Does it make even
our best utterances infallible? If not, by what
criterion are we to distinguish between the "inspiration" for which we pray and which we receive,
from that "inspiration"—the gift of an unction
from the Holy One—which was granted not only
to the Apostles and Evangelists, but to all baptized Christians? Dr. Cairns appeals to the prophecies and masterpieces which Scripture contains;
but these cannot possibly prove the co-extensive
miraculous inspiration of books and histories, and
poems which contain no such prophecy and no
such masterpieces, any more than the sublimest
passages of Milton's prose works, can defend from

criticism his plausible sophisms and savage invectives. The argument might indeed (as before) be reversed. "The Mosaic system," says Dr. Cairns, "was confessedly imperfect;" and the Bible contains "doctrinal difficulties and contradictions," to say nothing of ethical and scientific difficulties. Is it not just as fair, on the ground of "organic unity," to argue from these imperfections and difficulties against the thesis that "the Bible" *is* "the Word of God," as to argue, from the grander passages, that the entire book *is* the Word of God, and communicated by supernatural power? Mr. Mackennal, though he would not yield to Dr. Leathes or Dr. Cairns—any more than I would myself—in profound allegiance to the Holy Scriptures, and such intense reverence for them as more than justifies the devotion of every power to their elucidation, yet pronounces it "inconceivable" that the sacred writers should have applied to their ordinary narratives the description that they were "the Word of the Lord,"—a phrase which, as a matter of fact, they reserved for the highest and most special communications. In the papers of Mr. Mackennal and Mr. White we see the light of calm, independent judgment rising above dogmatic prepossessions to a clear grasp of truth. Undeceived by current phrases, which, except in a popular and general sense, are neither scriptural nor reasonably defensible, they have contributed to the discussion its chief element of originality and permanent value.

Professor Olver argues, as against Mr. Mackennal, that early Christian preachers (before a line of the New Testament was written) spoke of the Gospel as "the Word of God," and therefore that the New Testament may be so called. Certainly it may, but only *in the same general sense*. If it be maintained that even a St. Paul or a St. Peter, by using this phrase, claimed any supernatural infallibility for all their utterances, and for all their writings, the New Testament itself furnishes a sufficient refutation of so extravagant a proposition. It shows that even a Paul and a Peter, though they were "inspired men," *could* err and *did* err, both in their words and in their acts, during the very epoch that they were preaching "the Word of God," without detracting in any way from the weight of their essential witness to Christ. Thus the New Testament itself destroys the "organic unity" argument. Alike in the Old and New Testament we are guarded against the extravagant error of supposing that the imparting of the Holy Spirit was so total and so absolute as to give to all the words of any man a supernatural infallibility—a fallacy which seems to run through so much of the argument devoted to this topic. Samson was endowed with the Spirit of the Lord; David was still more highly endowed. Are we told to infer that the "organic unity" of their lives compels us to approve of all their acts or all their words? Does not the New Testament distinctly tell us that Apostle differed from Apostle, not, indeed, as regards their testimony to Christ, but yet as to practical opinions of great importance? What is it at which some of the writers aim? They argue for a rigid interpretation of the thesis that "the Bible *is* the Word of God," and yet, like Professor Olver, they say that even in the New Testament there is "a strange commingling of the ordinary and the extraordinary, of the natural and the supernatural." Apparently, too, the thesis has no applicability for ninety-nine hundredths of mankind, since we are cautioned that it does not apply to any wrong reading; or any interpretation, or any mistranslation; or, indeed (strictly speaking), to any translation at all; and, therefore, neither to our English Bible, nor to any but the original Hebrew and Greek. For, says Professor Olver, "Divine authority cannot be claimed for anything which is not a *correct translation of an exact copy of an originally authorised utterance and writing.*" Consequently, in spite of the "organic unity" which makes every chapter and verse and word of the Bible "the Word of God," nobody can be sure of any particular word or verse, since it may be an interpolation, like 1 John v. 7 and many small glosses; or a mistranslation like hundreds of passages in every current Bible; or even a non-canonical book like those of the Apocrypha; and in any case an ordinary man, without capacity or opportunity for a "scholarly criticism" and an "antiquarian research," cannot have the least security that what he reads in any particular passage is a correct translation of an exact copy, or even—in the face of differing canons—that it was "an originally authorised utterance and writing." Thus he can only decide at second hand, and from widely differing authorities, what *is* the Word of God!

Were it not better, without these mechanical theories and procrustean formulae, to speak to the people concerning the Bible more as follows?—The Bible is the book which contains the records of God's dealings with a chosen race, and through them with all mankind. Above all, it is the book which contains the gospel of His Son and the lessons of salvation. It is not all of the same value. It is not all written on the same level. It does not teach throughout the same morality. It contains some things which were permitted once "because of the hardness of men's hearts," but which are not permitted now. Much of it was addressed "to men of old time," which we have to supplement, to correct, and even to reverse. Much of it is occupied with the "weak and beggarly elements" of an obsolete bondage, "with statutes which were not good and judgments whereby they should not live." Much of it is written from the imperfect moral and spiritual standard of "times of ignorance" at which "God winked." You will find recorded in it, and recorded without comment or disapproval, some opinions and some actions, even of good men, which were not commendable. You will find attributed to God's command conduct which for us would now be heinously criminal. Nevertheless, this book is a sacred book, for the sum total and general drift of its teaching is loftier and diviner than you will find in any book in all the world. Both by its own loftiest utterances, and by the Christian conscience which it has trained, and by the final standard of its gospel, it furnishes you with ample means whereby to judge what things are right and wrong. The Spirit of God is with us still. The promise of that Spirit was not confined to the contemporaries of Pentecost, and His influences are living influences, and by them, throughout long ages, men have been slowly correcting the errors and the crimes for which their fathers have pleaded the sanction of the words of this book. By that Spirit of God you will be saved from the tyranny of a dead letter which might otherwise be to you, as it has been to thousands, a savour of death unto death. He will not in the least degree make you infallible or give the least authority to any assertion or opinion or definition or interpretation of yours about points respecting which Christians differ, but He will teach you all things which are necessary for your holiness here and your eternal happiness hereafter. Your Bible is no homogeneous whole which dropped down from heaven. It consists of sixty-six different books, the work of at least forty or fifty different writers, writing in different languages and dialects, and separated from each other by hundreds of years. It is not a book but a library* or a literature. Great parts of it are but the fragmentary wreck of a literature, from various

* See 2 Macc. ii. 13.

books of which—now no longer extant—many of its writers quote. The Old Testament, of which a considerable portion is by unknown authors, extends over a thousand years. It is separated by four hundred and fifty years from the New Testament. The translation of it is not always correct; the exact meaning is not always ascertainable; the text is not always certain; the meaning is not always clear; and the moral decisions which it contains are not always co-ordinate or comprehensible:—but all this is a matter of no essential importance, seeing that in this book, and above all in the Gospels, which record the life and teaching of the Saviour of the world, and in the Epistles of the greatest preachers of that Gospel you may find, not, indeed, a minute system about which you can dogmatise, or religious opinions which you can force on others with anathemas, but a moral and spiritual guidance which you cannot mistake. The end of the whole book is Christ. If it leads you to Christ its whole function is fulfilled. What is essential for rightly learning the way of salvation is not in the dead letter which may only kill, but in the spirit which giveth liberty and life. "Do not hear or read it for any other end but to become better in your daily walk, and to be instructed in every good work, and to increase in the love and service of God." *

It is obvious that it would require a volume to maintain and define all that I have said, but at any rate I have made clear the view which is not mine only, but has been in all ages the view of thousands and tens of thousands of the saints of God. In the Bible we hear the voice of God; in the Bible we may read the words of God; the Bible contains the messages of God to man. There is, therefore, nothing wrong or unintelligible in generally applying to the Bible, as a whole, that which is its most essential feature. Such a mode of speaking runs throughout the whole of our ordinary language. But when the term "the Word of God" is made co-extensive with every chapter of the Bible, and with all that it contains, the majesty of the phrase is at once degraded. It becomes dubious, if not unintelligible, when so used; it has been perverted into that dogma of absolute infallibility and plenary verbal inspiration, which—combined with the equal infallibility demanded for ignorant misapplications of the dogma—has in many an age filled the world with misery and ruin; which has done more than any

* Jeremy Taylor, "Holy Living," iv. 4.

other dogma to corrupt the whole of exegesis with dishonest casuistry, and to shake to its centre the religious faith of thousands, alike of the most ignorant and of the most cultivated in many centuries, and most of all in our own.

THE END.

LENTEN BOOKS.

CHURCH READER FOR LENT. A selection of forty-seven Readings from Modern Authors, adapted to use in Church Services or for private reading. 12mo, cloth. $1.25.

During the Lenten season many of the Clergy are so occupied that they find little time for preparing sermons. In view of the need of some helpful book, this collection of 47 Sermons has been carefully compiled and edited. They are from the collections by MacLaren, Buxton, Ewer, Grimley, Faber, Cross, and others, and will average only about ten minutes in delivery. They will also be found helpful for private reading.

SOME QUIET LENTEN THOUGHTS; being Meditations for the Forty Days of Lent. By T. BIRKETT DOVER, Vicar of St. Agnes, Kennington Park. With a Preface by Canon KING, of Oxford. 16mo, cloth. *Net*, 75 cents.

"We desire to commend most heartily to our readers' attention an admirable little book of daily meditations. Amongst their many great merits it may be said that they are short and therefore adapted for busy people. To mention, however, that they are recommended to Churchmen by the Rev. Dr. King, of Christ Church, who contributes a preface to the little volume, is to say all that is necessary to obtain the wide circulation they deserve."—*John Bull.*

GOOD FRIDAY. Addresses on the Seven Last Words. By Rev. H. S. HOLLAND, M.A., Canon of St. Paul's, author of "Logic and Life, with other Sermons." 16mo, cloth, red edges. 75 cents.

"They shed a new light on the Mystery of the Passion."—*The Church Standard.*

TOUCHSTONES; or Christian Graces and Characters Tested. By Rt. Rev. ASHTON OXENDEN, D.D. 16mo, neat cloth binding. 75 cents.

"One of those savory books for the soul which help in our spiritual life."—*The Observer.*

"It is plain, pithy, and full of good sense on points of common need and common failure in the Christian life."—*Standard of the Cross.*

THE SOWER. Six Lectures delivered in Lent, 1882. By Rev. ROBERT WILSON, M.D., D.D. Cloth, red edges. 75 cents.

"Rich in a wholesome spiritual teaching."—*The Pacific Churchman.*

Thomas Whittaker, 2 & 3 *Bible House, New York.*

CANON LUCKOCK'S NEW BOOK.

FOOTPRINTS OF THE SON OF MAN, as traced by St. Mark.

Being eighty portions for private study, family reading, and instruction in Church. By HERBERT MORTIMER LUCKOCK, D.D., author of "After Death," "Studies on the History of the Prayer Book," etc.; with an Introduction by the Lord Bishop of Ely. 2 vols., 12mo, cloth. $3.50.

REVELATION: UNIVERSAL and SPECIAL.

By Rev. W. W. OLSSEN, S.T.D., author of "Personality, Human and Divine." 12mo, cloth. $1.25.

THE APOCALYPSE OF ST. JOHN.

Self-interpreted for English readers, with a new translation. By Rev. SAMUEL FULLER, D.D., Professor in the Berkeley Divinity School. 12mo, cloth. $2.50.

After centuries of virtual exclusion from the Calendar, the Book of Revelation is now inserted in the Table of Lessons. The new position of the Book demands for it explanations "understanded of the people." In preparing his Commentary upon the inspired Book hereafter to be read in its completeness in all churches, the author strives to render intelligible to all classes of readers the teaching of Jesus Christ in its present application to His Church, in her incessant conflicts with error and sin, and especially in her duty, which she continually recognizes, "preach the Gospel to every creature." For the prompt, unremitted, and increasing obedience to this undying command of her Sovereign Lord, the Apocalypse presents the most constraining as well as the most encouraging motives.

BY THE SAME AUTHOR.

DEFENCE OF THE VERSION OF KING JAMES I, "The Spirits in Prison" (I *Peter* iii. 18-20), Against the Westminster Revision. 8vo, paper. 25 cents.

"My hope is that your pamphlet may find its way into the library of every clergyman and theological student in the American Church."
—*Bishop Beckwith.*

Thomas Whittaker, 2 & 3 *Bible House, New York.*

THE CHRISTIAN MINISTRY AT THE CLOSE OF THE NINETEENTH CENTURY.

THE BISHOP PADDOCK LECTURES, 1884.

By Rt. Rev. A. N. LITTLEJOHN, D.D., LL.D. Cantab., Bishop of Long Island. In one handsome octavo volume, cloth. $2.50.

CONTENTS:

I. THE CHRISTIAN MINISTRY AT THE BAR OF CRITICISM.
II. THE CAUSES THAT HAVE HINDERED or IMPAIRED THE INFLUENCE OF THE CHRISTIAN PRIESTHOOD.
III. EVIDENCES OF INTELLECTUAL VIGOR AND ACTIVITY IN THE MINISTRY.
IV. THE ACTIVITY OF THE CLERICAL OR THEOLOGICAL MIND IN CHRISTIAN AND SCIENTIFIC ETHICS.
V. INTELLECTUAL ACTIVITY OF THE CLERGY IN APOLOGETICS AND BIBLICAL CRITICISM.
VI. MATERIAL AND TRAINING FOR THE MINISTRY.
VII. PREACHING.
VIII. THE CLERGY AS EDUCATORS.
IX. IMPROVED METHODS IN THE CURE OF SOULS.
X. DOGMATIC TEACHING, AND THE PRIMARY ENDS OF THE GOSPEL.
XI. THE CHRISTIAN MINISTRY AND "THE NEW THEOLOGY."
XII. CHARACTER.

"They are very robust utterances, full of thought, and grandly practical in their tone, uncompromising in their convictions, loyal to a lofty ideal of ministerial character and work, and fitted to stimulate reflections, whether agreed to or not."—*The Literary World.*

"Nearly all the 'burning questions' of the present are gone over in these lectures."—*The Church.*

"Describes the limitations, defects and possibilities of the modern Christian ministry with great ability and truthfulness."—*New York Tribune.*

Thomas Whittaker, 2 & 3 *Bible House, New York.*

THE SPIRITS IN PRISON,

AND OTHER STUDIES ON THE LIFE AFTER DEATH. By E. H. PLUMPTRE, D.D., Dean of Wells. Small 8vo, cloth. $2.00.

"The book is certainly one of great and fascinating interest."—*The Church Eclectic.*

"It is a book for the time, and will find a widening circle of readers whose minds it will settle and whose faith it will strengthen and confirm."—*The Churchman.*

THE PROPHECIES OF ISAIAH.

A new Translation, with Commentary and Appendixes. By the Rev. T. K. CHEYNE, M.A. Third edition, revised. Two volumes in one. 8vo, cloth. $4.00.

"Mr. Cheyne's work is in many respects one of the most noteworthy of our day. . . . . He has been a devout and careful student of Isaiah for some 20 years past."—*N. Y. Times.*

"We rejoice that a Commentary which must be marked 'indispensable,' is thus put within the reach of a larger number of those who love the great prophet."—*Andover Review.*

"The qualities of Mr. Cheyne's Commentary would make it a good book in any language, or almost in any condition of Biblical learning. It is perspicuous without being superficial, and terse without the omission of anything of importance."—*Academy.*

Thomas Whittaker, 2 & 3 *Bible House, New York.*

I

THE CHRISTIAN SANCTIFIED BY THE LORD'S PRAYER. By the author of "The Hidden Life of the Soul," "Spiritual Maxims," etc. Translated from the French. 24mo, cloth, gilt edges. 50 cents.

"It is only the divers who find the pearls and the buried wealth of the sea; so it is only those who, in prayerful silence and solitude, search out the hidden things of God, who discover and disclose to us truths we should never otherwise have known. Thus Père Grou has revealed in this familiar prayer of our Lord a fulness, a richness, and a profound application to every human life, which gives it new beauty and power."—*From the Translator's Preface.*

II

THE CHARACTERISTICS OF TRUE DEVOTION. Translated from the French. 24mo, cloth extra. 60 cents.

"There are twenty-six brief chapters of instruction, remarkable for their direction, thoroughness, and simplicity."—*Living Church.*

"A very sweet and fragrant little volume, practical, and well adapted to all classes of Christians."—*Morning Star.*

"Excellent little volume, full of sweet, refreshing thoughts."—*Advocate and Guardian.*

PERSONAL PIETY. A Help to Christians to walk worthy of their Calling. By C. T. Fifth Edition. 24mo, cloth extra, red edges. 60 cents.

"As a gift to the newly confirmed it has special value."—*Dominion Churchman.*

"A very readable, excellent and timely little book."—*The Advocate and Guardian.*

Thomas Whittaker, 2 & 3 Bible House, New York.

The Gospel and the Age. Sermons on Special Occasions. By the Rt. Rev. W. C. MAGEE, D.D., D.C.L., Bishop of Peterborough. Third edition, small 8vo, cloth. $2.00.

"Will arrest the attention of the world."—*The Spectator.*
"Fine specimens of robust, manly eloquence."—*British Quarterly Review.*

Christian Truth and Modern Opinion. Seven Sermons by Clergymen of the Church. Fourth Edition. With a Preface by the Rt. Rev. HUGH MILLER THOMPSON, D.D. 12mo, cloth. $1.25.

CONTENTS:

THE CHRISTIAN DOCTRINE OF PROVIDENCE. By C. S. HENRY, D.D.
THE CHRISTIAN DOCTRINE OF PRAYER. By HUGH MILLER THOMPSON, D.D.
MORAL RESPONSIBILITY AND PHYSICAL LAW. By E. A. WASHBURN, D.D.
THE RELATION OF MIRACLES TO THE CHRISTIAN FAITH. By J. H. RYLANCE, D.D.
THE ONENESS OF SCRIPTURE. By W. R. HUNTINGTON, D.D.
IMMORTALITY. By Rt. Rev. THOMAS MARCH CLARK, D.D., LL.D.
EVOLUTION AND A PERSONAL CREATOR. By JOHN COTTON SMITH, D.D.

"The book is the outcome of reverent, honest, humble and scholarly men."—*Pulpit Treasury.*
"The fourth edition of this course of sermons comes none too soon for the times."—*The Church.*

The Apostles' Creed Tested by Experience. By Rev. C. R. BAKER. 12mo, cloth. 75 cents.

"The most striking feature in the present volume is in the adoption of a novel mode of dealing with the Creed and its lessons."—*New York Times.*

The Mystery of the Kingdom. Traced through the Four Books of Kings. Part I.—The First Book of Kings. By ANDREW JUKES. Third edition. 12mo, cloth. $1.00.

"The book merits the closest and most careful reading, for there is not a page which is not full of suggestiveness. . . . . Commended most heartily to the attention of teachers and students of Holy Scripture."—*The English Churchman.*

Thomas Whittaker, 2 & 3 *Bible House, New York.*

SPECIAL CHEAP EDITION.

THE PARAGRAPH TESTAMENT.

THE NEW TESTAMENT OF OUR LORD AND SAVIOUR JESUS CHRIST. THE AUTHORIZED EDITION IN PARAGRAPH FORM.—In this edition of the New Testament the publisher has omitted the divisions into *chapter* and *verse* (originally introduced by Robert Stephens, in connection with his Concordance), believing that, however convenient for citation, these divisions are superfluous and objectionable for general use. In other respects he has strictly adhered to the authorized English version, following the London edition in orthography and punctuation, except that he has availed himself of the use of *quotation points*, to mark distinct speeches, etc. For convenience of reference the *Index of Subjects*, from Bagster's edition, is appended. One handsome volume, crown octavo, 548 pages, new *Pica* type, fine cloth binding. 60 cents.

SOME CLERICAL OPINIONS.

" Taken as a whole, both as to arrangement and typography, I have no hesitation in saying that this edition is the best, for private uses, of any that I have seen."

" Your edition is in better print, and has several advantages of any other edition of the New Testament, based upon the received version."

" An excellent design excellently executed."

" This edition of the New Testament is in liberal type, unbroken into chapters and verses, but divided into paragraphs. The indications of the old divisions are placed at the head of the page. The release of the text from the fragmentary lacerations of the old verse system gives a new impression, both of more clearly connected meaning and a rounder and more complete style of the holy documents. We can not but believe that the obsolete method of verse division, which makes a sacred narrative or argument look like a series of select sentences, interrupting the thought and losing the true connections, will be abandoned."—*From the Quarterly Review.*

Thomas Whittaker, 2 & 3 *Bible House, New York.*

New Juvenile Books.

FOR SUNDAY-SCHOOL LIBRARIES AND HOME READING.

LOVEDAY'S HISTORY. A Tale of Many Changes. By LUCY ELLEN GUERNSEY. 12mo. $1.50.

GOLD AND GLORY; OR, WILD WAYS OF OTHER DAYS. A Tale of Early American Discovery. By GRACE STEBBING, author of "Only a Tramp." 12mo. $1.50.

THE CHILDREN'S PILGRIMAGE. By L. T. MEADE, author of "David's Little Lad," "Scamp and I," etc. 12mo. $1.50.

ANNA CAVAYE; OR, THE UGLY PRINCESS. By SARAH DOUDNEY, author of "Nothing but Leaves," etc. 12mo. $1.25.

WALTER ALISON, HIS FRIENDS AND FOES. By M. L. RIDLEY, author of "The Three Chums." 12mo. $1.00.

DOROTHY. A Tale. By T. M. BROWNE, author of "Not my Way." 12mo. $1.00.

CASTLE COMFORT. A Story for Children. By Mrs. W. J. HAYS, author of "The Princess Idleways," "A Domestic Heroine," etc. 12mo. $1.00.

CLIFFORD'S TRIAL; OR, THE CONQUEST OF PATIENCE. By YOTTY OSBORN. 12mo. $1.25.

THE THREE CHUMS. By M. L. RIDLEY, author of "Our Captain. $1.00.

STORIES FROM ENGLISH HISTORY. By LOUISA CREIGHTON. With numerous Illustrations. 12mo. $1.25.

"NOT MY WAY;" OR, GOOD OUT OF EVIL. A Story. By T. M. BROWNE. 12mo. $1.00.

A LOVING SISTER. A Story for Big Girls. By Mrs. W. J. HAYS. 12mo. $1.00.

GRACE DARLING; THE HEROINE OF THE FARNE ISLES. By EVA HOPE. 12mo. $1.00.

GETTING TO BE WOMEN. By GEORGE KLINGLE. 12mo. $1.25.

Thomas Whittaker, 2 & 3 *Bible House, New York.*

www.ingramcontent.com/pod-product-compliance
Lightning Source LLC
Chambersburg PA
CBHW021359230426
43666CB00006B/576